The Cost of Dying

AND WHAT YOU CAN DO ABOUT IT

RAYMOND PAAVO ARVIO

The Cost of Dying

AND WHAT YOU CAN DO ABOUT IT

HARPER & ROW, PUBLISHERS

NEW YORK, EVANSTON, SAN FRANCISCO, LONDON

1817

FIRST EDITION

Designed by Sidney Feinberg

Library of Congress Cataloging in Publication Data

Arvio, Raymond Paavo.
    The cost of dying and what you can do about it.
    Includes bibliographical references.
    1. Undertakers and undertaking—United States.
2. Consumer education. I. Title.
HD9999.U53U52   1974   338.4'7'6146097   74–4629
ISBN 0–06–060305–4

Contents

Acknowledgments

When the Rockland County, New York, Memorial Society entrusted me with the job of Secretary-Treasurer many years ago, I had no idea that the experience of aiding and counseling members to plan their funerals in advance would link itself with an older and deeper love: the cooperative movement. This book joins the two strands of thought and interest into a proposal for a nationwide response to conditions in the funeral marketplace. Through self-help and mutual-aid techniques, consumers can provide themselves with a measure of control over their own economic and social destinies.

Isabelle L. Roeandt, the president of our memorial society, permitted me full range of thought and action, as we both labored to add members to our little group. Mae Lahti, my mother, who performed the many office and administrative tasks basic to a group's growth, contributed cheerfully and in countless ways to our progress. Jenifer Schroeder, for many years the effective Executive Secretary of the Continental Association of Funeral and Memorial Societies, and Ernest Morgan, whose dedication to funeral reform is so clear in his unique *Manual for Death Education and Simple Burial,* are among the many people who provided an atmosphere of inspiration and search for new answers.

I am grateful for the faith of the fathers and mothers of the cooperative movement, who, like my own, believed that a New World could be built if people would only work together. The continuing labor and dedication of brothers and sisters I know among housing co-ops, in food stores, in credit unions and in other cooperative institutions have always kept my own faith alive, and I thank them all.

To Cynthia Arvio, my partner for twenty-three years, who used her poetic love of words and keen editing skills to help me sharpen the impact of the book, I give thanks. I appreciate, too, the support and faith of those faculty members and students at Queens College who, caught up in the idea of reform, organized the Queens Memorial Society.

In June 1973 the Memorial Society of New Hampshire through its president, Ann Doak, invited me to appear on television on a Friday and to speak to its annual meeting on a Sunday. The free Saturday they provided, in the Finland-like atmosphere of the New England Center for Continuing Education—a truly civilized set of structures mounted in the rocks and woods—gave me an ideal setting for the first construction of an orderly and meaningful plan for the handling of death.

RAYMOND PAAVO ARVIO

Introduction

A specter haunts the American funeral today.

It is the specter of enlightened consumerism.

A gentle flow of public and private criticism over the years has been tolerated by the powerful funeral Establishment, while Jessica Mitford,[1] Ruth Mulvey Harmer[2] and Leroy Bowman[3] are dismissed as hopeless radicals. The funeral director bridles slightly when confronted by the names of these critics and then changes the subject. These people have been flies in his ointment, mere annoyances to his view of himself as a man of high calling, a true servant.

But criticism is moving toward action. And that troubles the funeral director and his colleagues. Why? Because consumers now are beginning to see American funerals with the same critical eye with which they view their purchases in supermarkets, in automobile display rooms, in real estate offices, in the hundred relationships they have in the marketplace.

There is good sense in the consumer's logic. The cost of funerals is rising rapidly. In some communities, many funeral directors "begin" at $1,000. It is hard to avoid $2,000 and $3,000 funerals, when the costs of added services, grave plots, flowers and other items are included. The complex emotions of grief and guilt are skillfully parlayed by the Establishment into expensive occasions, using money that might be better used for the living.

The consumer is just becoming aware that the funeral director is not merely a local friendly citizen, serving the needs of neighbors and friends, but part of a hard-hitting, well-organized, well-financed lobby, whose network of trade associations, of legislative lobbyists and lawyers strives to maintain the hold the funeral director has on the market and, of course, on the consumer's personal fortune. Antagonism of the funeral industry to consumer-protection legislation and regulation is not merely intellectual; it is substantial and effective opposition.

Most state regulatory bodies supervising funeral industries are composed of funeral directors. Few states have protective legislation for consumers. There is none at the federal level.

The minutes of the proceedings of the 1972 San Diego, California, gathering of the Continental Association of Funeral and Memorial Societies were in the hands of New York funeral lobbyists before they had even reached member societies of the Association. Nothing, no challenge to their leadership, goes unnoticed. Their apprehension is mounting.

The consumer is aware, too, that the funeral industry is using its energy to forestall any substantial advances at the educational level. Under the guidance of one of its national trade groups, funeral directors are engaged in a systematic approach to schools and colleges, offering programs in "death education" and substantial amounts of literature, all designed to show Americans that the funeral directors are providing a valuable service, that they are a respected profession, that their concern is pure service. Their concern, they allege, is to help young people understand and accept death. In reality, the programs are designed to underline dependence on the current mode of funeral practices. Garbed in unctuous and sentimental language, the educational literature is designed to serve the need of the trade to forestall the growing pattern of criticism.

It is not the purpose of this document to add to the literature of funeral criticism. Funeral practices are already under the scrutiny of writers and students of the field. Consumer organizations increasingly show awareness in this field. Memorial societies grow in numbers and strength, reflecting a greater understanding of actual conditions in the funeral marketplace.

This book is designed to provide encouragement, practical advice and guidance for nonprofit memorial societies, for religious organizations, for consumer organizations and for consumers.

It will not belabor more than is necessary the practices of the private-profit practitioners in the field, but some comparisons will need to be made from time to time. It will assume the right of consumers to organize and to control their own destiny. The argument for self-help and mutual aid will be stated forthrightly, with practical suggestions on the proper conduct and spirit of a cooperative organization. Human and business problems that must be overcome will be discussed in some detail.

In some senses, of course, the book is a manifesto, calling for accelerated social change from an advanced point of view through the creation of new institutions.

The specter, not so fearsome after all when examined clearly, which faces the private-profit funeral industry is that consumers will, through various mechanisms and devices, displace private profit with programs based on service, on the stated and educated needs of consumers—and, of course, of their survivors.

It is not utopian to envision new institutions. Some already exist. More are in the planning stages. Many consumers are rapidly coming to the conclusion that private industry needs the corrective of direct competitive challenge.

Under these circumstances, tools are needed. It is hoped that this book will encourage explorations and that it will assure those who struggle with the thought that massive social change is not only desirable, a point on which pioneers already agree, but that it is possible.

RAYMOND PAAVO ARVIO

September 1974
Pomona, New York

Invitation to Readers

Readers of *The Cost of Dying* are invited to respond to the propositions I raise, to share experiences, to reflect on its contents, to probe future directions.

A mighty conversation of thousands of consumers must be heard throughout the land if change is to occur. Perhaps this book can play a part.

I can be reached at Route 45, Pomona, New York 10970.

RAYMOND PAAVO ARVIO

The Cost of Dying

AND WHAT YOU CAN DO ABOUT IT

The Future
of Death

1

The note from Aunt Jane in Milwaukee said that Uncle Charlie had died suddenly. Knowing of our interest in funeral practices, she told us that his various organs had been made available to six people who needed body-part replacements. In addition, she said there was time for a corneal transplant. Aunt Jane had even visited with the newly sighted person. "I'm so happy," she said, "to know that Charlie's eyes have been put to good use by others." Through her sadness, she seemed proud.

The station wagon turned in at the driveway marked simply, BODY RECYCLING CENTER. Driving down the tree-lined lane, Mrs. Mobley glanced from side to side, viewing the lush greenery.

The distant yellow brilliance of the spring-blooming forsythias was counterpoised against rows of dark pines. The lawn that reached down to the driveway guided her eyes to the distant reception facility perched on a gentle hill.

Approaching slowly, her car followed the arrows that pointed to the INTAKE parking lot. Drawing the car to a halt in an open parking spot, unleashing her seat belt, she stepped out of the car. She took a glance at the rear of the car. Wrapped in a sheet was the body of her husband, Charles. "I've brought him here myself," she thought.

Her sons had offered to take his body to the Center. But she told

1

them she wanted to do it herself. Mrs. Mobley walked to the office door. A few minutes later, two men came out with a cart. Opening the rear door of the station wagon, they reached for the body, pulled it out, placed it gently in the cart and wheeled it off to another entryway into the building.

Mrs. Mobley left the office before long. She had filled out the necessary forms and now she was returning home, alone. Driving through the parklike atmosphere, she knew what would happen to Edward's body. It would be planted, "like a seed," she mused, in one of the park's newer sections. Some years from now, the topsoil of that section would be available for gardens in the municipal parks. Householders, too, could come for bags of the human compost, the rich new soil, for their flower gardens. It was a comforting notion for Mrs. Mobley. The couple had always liked flowers and shrubbery and their own gardens were a neighborhood pride. Now Edward would himself enrich yet other gardens.

In a grove of trees some distance from the city, the Life-to-Life Center buzzed with its twenty-four-hour-a-day activity. Delivery trucks eased into their ramps, workers then unloading bodies one at a time onto a moving conveyor belt. The trucks, emptied, fired up again, leaving for a return trip to the city's Body Collection Centers. It was a never-ending process. So long as people died, the Life-to-Life Center would be busy.

The conveyors slid the naked bodies into the Disposition Room, where two attendants took each body, placed it on a cart which held five or six bodies. The cart was wheeled into a Drying Room. Six such rooms were constantly in operation. When several dozen carts were in one of the rooms, its capacity reached, the outer door was closed and the heat-process began. At the right moment, the dehumidified bodies were wheeled, still on their carts, into the Dust Room. Passed into processing machines, the bodies became pure dust. Pure energy. Fed into cloth sacks in adjoining work-rooms, the human dust was soon to be on its way to the nation's farm lands.

In the old days, people remembered, a body would be wasted. It would be placed in a coffin and buried in a cemetery, useless. But international shortages of food had prompted rethinking. Life had a responsibility to life, it had been argued in those distantly remembered debates. One by one, advanced nations had rejected the old ways and made it possible for the dead bodies of their citizens to contribute to the life of others.

On the farms, the bags would be unloaded on distribution machines, which would move back and forth along clearly defined rows and drop the fine powder along the soil's ridges. Turned over by yet other machines, the soil would produce a good harvest of food for the giant and hungry cities of the world.

High on the twenty-second floor of a high-rise apartment building in an eastern city, a doctor was busy with his patient.

From time to time he left the bedroom, where his patient lay quietly, to confer with relatives in the living room. At one point, at his call, the relatives entered the bedroom. They gathered around the bed. Ben's last struggle with life was over. One by one, sadly, the relatives left the bedroom, joining the others in the living room. The doctor called the coroner's office.

A representative from the coroner's came in half an hour, having received in his car radio news of a death. He entered the bedroom, confirmed Ben's death. He signed some papers.

One of the relatives called the maintenance room and reported the death. The body, the porter was told, would be deposited in the building's incinerator chute in about ten minutes. Two of the stronger relatives wrapped Ben's lifeless body in the blanket which had kept him warm earlier, while the others watched. Lifting up his body, the two balanced themselves carefully for a moment and then proceeded slowly toward the apartment door.

Followed by the relatives and distantly by the doctor and the coroner's representative, the procession quietly went down the hallway to the incinerator room. There, the chute door was opened and the body eased in.

Back in the apartment, having thanked the doctor and the coroner's representative, both of whom had received beeper calls and knew they were needed elsewhere, the relatives sat back and talked together about Ben's life. A gathering of Ben's friends was planned for later that week.

The uplifted eye, on a clear cloudless night, could almost imagine the green fields of the moon. Though it was too far away really to reveal color, the once-lifeless dry moon had come to life. It was a moon of milk and honey. Harvest on harvest of life-giving corn, wheat, an endless variety of grains and fresh vegetables, flown to Earth on daily load-bearing missiles, assured mankind its daily bread.

It had started when the scientist Selden Breitsprecher realized, after countless experiments with moon-soil (moon-dust, really) that massive doses of organic substance could create a soil useful for the production of food for the crowded planet Earth. Specialized plant-breeding experiments produced species that could manage in the strange air of the moon.

At first, chemical fertilizers had been blasted, via Cape Kennedy's facilities, to the moon work-staff. However, the agricultural specialists were disappointed with the results. Dr. Breitsprecher's insights changed the focus: animal manures were sent up, but a world shortage of natural fertilizers caused that experiment to be discontinued.

His persistent genius hit on the idea of using the unwanted dead bodies of mankind. Dead mankind could help feed live mankind! For a year, every child knew from his classroom reading, the Good Doctor worked night and day in his laboratories. His conclusion was unavoidable: the moon would come to life, its deserts would bloom, if the earth's bodies could be sent to the moon for simple burial. There, after a period of time, the bodies would decompose, enriching the dust.

Now, from a hundred launching pads, located in key areas of the planet, regular delivery schedules sent bodies to the moon. The missiles returned with food.

Unlikely developments?

Possibly.

But we have experienced and come to accept other changes.

There have been those who said we should not tamper with the capitalist system, yet our societies went on to accept the liberal and humanitarian view of the state as a beneficent provider and source of security. There have been those who laughed at (even scorned) the idea of Social Security, the right of every citizen to a decent life and a decent retirement. Yet that idea has been implemented, in some measure, in most human societies today.

Airplanes came out of our inventive brains, despite the warnings of those who said that for a divine reason we had been created without wings. That words and pictures could fly invisibly through the air seemed to older generations the rantings of madmen. Oil and coal produced their wonders. Molds produced life-saving miracle drugs.

Shall we accept the inevitability of cancer? Or shall the "mad" scientists of our time keep peering into their microscopes, patiently certain that one of them will find the solution? In fact, we have become so accustomed to changes that we firmly believe the causes of cancer will be discovered, because other dread troubles have caused us misery, then become only a memory, in our own lifetimes. Poliomyelitis and other cripplers and killers of children are past nightmares. Even the wrinkling of old age and the troubles that old flesh is heir to will meet their masters, and maybe we'll live longer. We live in the age of hope realized.

We are in the midst of history being made, a Living History. We have overcome mysteries which, once exposed, become in a short time commonplace understandings to anyone who talks with friends, listens to the radio, reads a newspaper. Indeed, there is so much information available now about so many things that the all-capable Renaissance man of a few centuries ago just could not exist among us; no one can know everything there is to know, no one can do everything there is to do. Our specialization into disciplines, into narrow fields of work is the natural result of expanded knowledge. Each of us bites into only one corner of the enlarged borders of Truth.

Formerly sacred institutions like marriage and the home are under constant scrutiny, not only by troubled or inquisitive or adventurous people but by our popular literature. Even scholars have entered the picture. A professional class has arisen to lead us in our rethinking.

The male of the species is also under attack for his leadership at the expense of the female. We probe our psyches, our feelings, our moods in countless experiments. The last frontiers of the mind, our most private selves, are conquered by spiritual Conestoga wagons. Nothing is sacred. Or are we saying in some utterly divine, logical, new and beautiful way that we are making everything sacred, special to the gods and to ourselves?

Only one institution seems to remain untouchable, deeply and firmly bred into our consciousness: the funeral system, the way we in our Western societies dispose of our dead bodies.

Despite our new openness, we would rather not discuss death. (Now, if someone could help us to live forever . . . we could talk forever.) As in all other areas of human experience, change comes only when enough people believe . . . know . . . that there are answers. Unfortunately, death will not go away (not yet at least). Changes are coming, however, as one person after another squares up to the challenge, tries out ideas on friends and a new movement of thought begins.

Whatever qualities we might give to discussions of death, we often call such talk, in a kind of instant judgment, morbid. Or depressing. However, we have overcome our hesitations enough to accept the idea of life insurance. We do fight death through support of scientific innovation to keep life going. Certainly we believe in the beneficence of good medicine. We are concerned about automobile safety. We are "will conscious" increasingly, knowing the problems facing those who die intestate. Death figures in our calculations, but we don't call it death.

Death itself? We stop there. That is too personal, too much. "Could we discuss something else?"

Philosophically, the unwillingness to face death as a life question may seem to be part of an unreal view of life. Do we believe we are going to live forever? We must learn to accept the inevitability of death. I am going to die. You, my friend, are going to die.

Now, those words said, we can begin living.

We can begin asking questions.

We can begin to look at how death is handled in our society. No; we must say, rather, how *our* deaths are handled.

Our historic unwillingness to look at our death practices has contributed to the development of a multi-billion-dollar industry, a private-profit sales-and-service enterprise whose unchallenged preempting of an entire field of service may be unparalleled in human experience. Seldom have so few exploited so many, with so few critics and reformers, from either within or without. The fine and decent men in the funeral field, who entered out of genuine concern to serve others, are quiet voices in an industry gone awry. They seem unable to right the balance in a business that has become excessively commercial and crass.

That ceremony should accompany death is understandable. Funerals seem necessary to our human condition. Death is a moment in time that needs recognition. The loss is irretrievable. We must weep and we must laugh.

Our natural feelings of grief and guilt at the time of death, rendering us helpless before the onslaught of people making money on our misery, have blinded us to the transformation of the simple acknowledgment and celebration of life and death into an ornate catering operation. Everyone becomes a King at his funeral. Complicating our own intellectual and emotional problems with the question of death has been the emergence of black-suited, somber merchants, who have told us not to worry, that they will take care of all the details. With such reassurances comes a collapse of any questioning we might have wished to pursue.

It is not ceremony itself that is coming under judgment in the latter half of the twentieth century. It is that the understandable need for ceremony has led to abuse. When consumers stop to think about it, they realize that the major portion of the large funeral bill is for merchandise. One can argue that the time spent, the personal service provided by the funeral director and his staff, deserves to be paid for. They are, after all, doing the things we do not want to do ourselves. But the rest is coffins, hardware, pillows, mattresses. Soft goods. Hard goods. And sales resistance at the time of death is understandably low, especially if there has been no advance planning.

No purchase is made under comparable stresses. No one buys a car while filled with the raging emotions of grief and guilt. Nor a house. Not even life insurance. Nothing. Funeral directors, because of these stresses and the usual lack of planning, have been able to push merchandise a calmer mind might disavow, to create an instant need for goods through the use of the usual sales techniques, to foster status-reaching. They can discourage otherwise stubborn consumers from any orientation toward low expense. The sale of merchandise is the goal. For it is in such sales that the greatest profit lies.

Also, for its own ends, this ceremony-providing Estate that we call the funeral industry has wrapped a strange cloak of divine necessity about it. The modern American funeral, extravagant, cruel, crude and expensive, is now cloaked with the mantle of the American flag and blessed with Scripture. Thus critics can be called troublemakers or even communists. And questioning, perhaps just beginning, is stopped in its tracks.

New Trends

But there are observable new trends in community thought and experience that will have their effect on the funeral industry. Now the last fixed star in our old firmament of values, the American funeral, has been challenged. Criticized by Bowman, Mitford, Harmer and others, the funeral industry confronts a citizenry more aware than ever before. The reluctance to discuss death and death practices is diminishing ever so slightly as popular literature, columnists, thought-leaders pick up the tune begun by the pioneer critics. The question of course is, "Will enough consumers take the matter seriously, personally?"

Criticism does not necessarily lead to change. Americans sometimes settle for the act of criticism, as if it were enough, as if some inspired democratic magic would prompt the necessary changes. We are patient, too patient consumers and criticism is often the last desperate act. To move beyond criticism seems a burden, an unwanted involvement. Passive acceptance of the abuses in the marketplace has characterized the consumer. Complain, yes. "But what can you do?" We have a thousand consumer equivalents of "You can't fight City Hall."

Mitford's book in particular, *The American Way of Death,* came as a crusader's lance. On her white horse, Mitford rattled the armor of the funeral industry. Her criticism brought to some citizens, who "always knew something was wrong with funerals," a sense of righteousness. "Isn't it good that someone has written about it?"

There is the possibility, too, given our American propensities, that some people thought the questions had been settled for them and for American society. Surely some government agency was now keeping an eye on funeral directors. Accepting again the false idea that to criticize is to change, they failed to see that few changes had occurred. Thoughtful people were certainly pleased that someone had dared to buck the Establishment; meanwhile, back in hometown America, the local funeral parlor continued its work in its way. Funeral directors wince when, in rare circumstances, the Mighty Name of Mitford is raised, mutter something about "that communist," and then move on to make the arrangements and sell the merchandise that bring in the essential cash.

Mitford-influenced citizens have asked too few questions. The backbones of people were not straightened enough by her hard criticisms. The live citizen in the funeral parlor, making arrangements for the disposal of the body of a dead citizen, caught up in private feelings, pressed on by the need for quick decision-making, unwilling yet to ask the critical questions that might make a difference in the funeral and in the cost, continues the practices of generations before. Change is yet to come, pie-in-the-sky waits for another time.

The honorable liberal notion that Education . . . Enlightenment . . . leads automatically to progress falls apart in the actual experience of people. Information alone does not necessarily provide the will that might be necessary. We have all the information we need about the practices of funeral directors; we lack the will and courage to function differently.

Perhaps we're cowards because we do not have a vision of what new behavior could be. Criticism rarely outlines the new world; that task is left to the utopians, the dreamers, the planners. Just what else *would* I do? Just what else *could* I do? Can things be different? are questions that must be asked and answered if information is to lead into new patterns of behavior.

Critics educate us, certainly. They provide the stuff of our arguments pro and con all kinds of issues. But what *are* the next steps, cry outraged Americans? Where do we go from here?

The Impact of Consumerism

People today move in an environment of "consumerism," the movement of thought seeking to help men and women control their own fate in the marketplace. Aroused by the work of critics such as

Ralph Nader who want the present "system" to work, by the work of the cooperativists, the organizers, the reformers, the alternative-system people, the consumer activists, people today are asking if they have received their money's worth. Consumer rights have become politically attractive, too, as politicians acquire votes through their advocacy.

More than ever before, consumers read labels. They ask questions of store managers. They demand information, to inform their buying. They write letters. They respond to "hot-line" opportunities in the commercial media. They subscribe in increasing numbers to the non-profit *Consumer Reports*,[1] and also read private-profit consumer-advice publications like *Changing Times*,[2] *Money*,[3] *Moneysworth*[4] and others. Few industries have been spared: insurance, housing, auto-mobiles, food distribution, clothing, appliances and home furnishings, health care delivery—all have had their stances and performances modified by informed consumers and perceptive government consumer-protection agencies. Professional rip-offs are being challenged by doctors themselves, by dentists who tell the inside story (between tooth-pullings). The complaint orientation grows. "Speak up," we are urged.

At first consumerism, in the minds of many, dealt with problems of food and food distribution. That is understandable since food is such an everyday necessity. The movement into other fields was slow, but the tide eventually washed in. It is just beginning to include the hitherto untouched funeral, as consumers become aware that no field should be spared a hard analysis.

New Organizations

In addition to the gradually developing consumer consciousness through which individuals can opt for justice for themselves, new strengths are being found in organization. The Consumers Union of the U. S.,[5] the granddaddy membership organization with skill in product research and testing and the lonely public spokesman for so many years, has been supplemented by a new breed of activity, the voluntary association of consumers in new groups. With foci on consumer education, on various forms of action, on legislative lobbying, the local, state or regional consumer assemblies provide an opportunity for people to work together.

Existing groups are finding new thrusts, too. Trade unions, for example, traditionally oriented toward wage and working conditions, are discovering a "consumer interest." It is politically attractive, perhaps desirable, for these groups and their leadership to recognize the needs of consumers as part of their total program. Their own members are consumers, too. Wage gains at the lathe, won hard at the bargaining table, are easily lost in an unrestrained, untempered marketplace.

At the national level, the Consumer Federation of America,[6] even though it has no provision for individual memberships, has made it possible for more than two hundred consumer and consumer-interest groups to lobby jointly in Washington, D.C., long the sole territory and private hunting preserve of manufacturing and commercial interests.

Even brave organizations will rarely move ahead of their constituencies. Funeral reform will not be a high priority until a sizable consumer opinion on the subject has been expressed. And the development of such an opinion in the funeral field will not be a simple task.

Change Is
Not Easy

2

Our fascination with death is strong. We peer into crashed automobiles and at bloodied bodies lying in the street. We read, with eyes agog, of events surrounding the death of great personages and their funerals. It is not just that we are fascinated by the lives of the rich and the powerful: we are also curious about death. The debate about the actual number of bullets to penetrate the assassinated President Kennedy's brain continues, amidst charges and countercharges that vital information has been suppressed. How the picture of the slain Kent State College student, with a co-ed leaning over his body, stays with us! The physical condition of former President Truman was broadcast nationally, as he lay in a hospital bed during his last days. We stare mutely at war photos trying, perhaps, to comprehend the significance of death. The atom-bomb cloud, the modern symbol of wholesale killing, has burned itself indelibly into our brain cells.

War is not a part of the daily experience of Americans, so death by gunfire, napalm and dropping bombs is not imminent and personal. The highways and their horrid death tolls may be the closest we have come to the war experience of, say, the Vietnamese, who have known a state of war for forty years or more.

We can and do discuss other people's deaths. But to discuss our own is to plunge into raging seas, to do things differently. We would rather believe as we act, that we shall indeed live forever.

Of course, if substantial change is to occur in the funeral marketplace, there will need to be a willingness among consumers not only to discuss death more openly but also to function differently. Death practices do not change of themselves.

New practices will not just appear, full-blown, out of the heads of reformers. Everyday people will need convincing.

The trouble right now is that we resist change.

Death is, after all, intimate. It has to do with "me." That is what makes the subject threatening.

We recognize the reality of death, but we don't see it naturally. Our largely urban lives have been spared the anguish of death, but we have also missed the awareness of life's bright and dark cycles experienced by even the most obtuse farmer. The child on a farm where animals are raised may be more in tune with life's cycles than the oldest city-worn grandfather. A dog gives birth. Chicks are hatched. Mama Duck arrives with her waddling ones. A cow gives life to its young. Death of an animal requires a hole dug in the back field. Meat animals or chickens, having been sold to the market, have a certain destiny at the end of their truck-trip. City people have been exempted from such wholesome experiences, wholesome because of the acceptance and understanding of the life-death cycle and relationship which arise under these circumstances.

Children everywhere, on the farm and in the city, are usually spared human funeral experiences. This is unfortunately a denial of the need for life education. "He is too young, he won't understand, leave him home," is an often heard bit of friendly advice at funeral time in distressed households, as the family prepares to leave for the grim occasion at the funeral parlor. But this unprepared child will have to see to the funerals of his friends and parents in later years. We keep ourselves from thinking about death, and we keep the cycle of ignorance turning and turning by keeping the subject from our children. "To spare them," we say, but what a cruel deception!

So Who's Denying Death?

The underlying mental reality for most consumers and most members of the Funeral Establishment, the embrace which joins them both, is the unwillingness to accept death.

But that's silly, you say. Deny death?

Most funeral activity, as we know it today, is death-denying.

We would like to forget death, hoping that, if we just look in another direction, paint another picture of it, function in a certain way, it will go away.

Of course, death doesn't go away. It doesn't escalate, it doesn't diminish. Slow and steady, it wins every race sooner or later.

The Funeral Establishment isn't responsible for our tendency to deny death. They do exacerbate the tendency in us, feed on it, nurture it, because there's money in it, a livelihood. And directors are people, too.

Consumers and funeral directors alike deny death.

When consumers change, when their buying resistance is stronger, when their standards are different, the funeral people will have to accommodate. Right now it's a honeymoon. Everything is sweet. But, as it is in marriage, there will be changes.

Death-denying, in its ultimate sense, is that complex of practices which keeps the body from joining the natural elements of the earth as quickly after death as possible, by preserving and encasing remains, by niche-ing ashes, by memorializing on wood and stone and metal the names and existences of persons long-gone, which has institutionalized our grief and guilt into a buying orgy of tremendous proportions to seek relief from the too clear vistas of the inevitable.

Sensing that most consumers (like themselves) want to avoid the reality of death, funeral directors, alert to their prey, have responded with absurd gaud. Embalming nourishes the idea that the body will remain in perfect condition in the ground, not decaying; painting the face adds to the feeling that the person will remain as he was in life; hermetically sealed coffins (alleged to stall decay from inrushing ground water, worms and so on) lend further false assurance; containers for the underground coffins (to avoid decomposition of the coffin!) keep up the illusion; comfortable coffins (with innerspring mattresses) press a harder and more incomprehensible point. Columbaria to store the ashes in costly niches, for occasional family pilgrimages, avoid the reality of death and the ultimate union of ashes with the soil. Mausoleums and crypts do the same.

It is fashionable for funeral directors who have thought about it and for those who espouse the directors' cause to criticize reformers as death-denying, alleging that their opposition is to funerals as such. The fact is that few if any reformers in the funeral field are against ceremony. Death is a mark in time which makes its mark on us. The burial itself is a mark. What reformers oppose is the building up of the ceremony (i.e., the funeral) into a gigantic, costly mockery of sentiment, when moods and needs are exploited for the sake of selling merchandise. Positive in spirit, the reformers propose responsible alternatives to the current spending wave.

Probing Our Resistance

Enlightened consumers willing to venture into funeral reform need to recognize that behind the stillness of many consumers there is a complex of feelings, experiences and attitudes which must be understood if change is to occur.

Why do so many consumers whose support will be needed resist change in the funeral field?

There are many reasons.

1. The Idea of Death Itself Is Unacceptable

Everything possible is done to avoid exposure to natural death. The elderly are hidden away from view, discards in the back rooms of our homes or, more likely, in institutions away from family and public view. Our public concern for conditions in these old-age warrens is minimal. To become aware of the life the elderly must actually live, whether they are happy or sad, among friends or lonely, well or disabled, is to stare at the inevitability of our own deaths.

"I don't want to think about it," is the gut reaction of most people. Who *wants* to? To reflect on death is to recall the sadness, the grief of some loss. Who wants to reawaken memories of the loss of a parent, or a lover or a good friend? To think about death is to readmit feelings of deep distress, memories of sobbing over the loss of a parent after a long and good life, the death of a child from a killer-disease, the accidental loss of a young friend on the highway. These deep channels of memory may also be muddied by legal and family complications we have known. If we are silent, maybe such thoughts will go away.

To consider the possibility of death is also to evaluate life. People are aware of the waste and uselessness of much of their lives, their fruitless work, their unrewarding leisure. Failure stalks our innards. Death, staring you in the eyes, so to speak, looks at your whole life. Many people are not satisfied with their lives. They don't know how to change their patterns, don't want to, or can't. Their usual passive submission and acceptance of what life has provided are shaken when thoughts focus on its being all over.

If life seems rich and full, the thought of death is also troubling. "I'm having such a helluva good time that I don't want to think about it ending," cries the *bon vivant.*

Thinking about death also reawakens old rejected religions. Emancipated from their traditions, many feel guilt nevertheless about their abandonment of religious values and institutions which they identify with their parents. Their own historic identity is tightly linked with the religions-that-were.

That we felt bad when we said no to Mama and Papa's ways is clear. We have tried to forget how bad we felt. Most of the associations we happen to have with death are cultural-religious associations, occasions out of our dim past we would soon enough forget, if we could. The sensation of guilt about leaving old pasts is strongest in those who have not found satisfying life-views of their own, the millions who live in religious and philosophical limbos of their own making. Trying to survive the years of their lives without the certainties of their past, they have built no alternatives; they have merely blocked out the past. "If I don't think about it, maybe it'll go away." But it doesn't, and it is easily revived.

Traditional religion provides an easy approach to death. "I will see my son again," says the mother on the untimely death of her child, confident that her simple faith will come true. The comforting idea of reunion of families after death met the needs of many and continues to do so. To reject the pieties and practices of those orthodoxies is also to leave oneself in a void. Death-thoughts for those who have left their past behind make it all too clear that no substitute has been provided. "My folks had the answer to death, and it reassured them. I don't have any answers. I only know death comes." And again, "I don't want to think about it."

2. *Death Suggests an Order to Life*

The kind of panic that pushes people from one day into the next, the busy round of activities, trying to pay bills, trying to raise kids, worrying about job security, are features of an environment that resists planning. There's almost no time to plan! The sense of dissatisfaction with one's lifework, the general environment, political and social progress (the little there is) is heightened when systematic discussion about death is urged.

Death, being certain, argues for recognition, for planning. One knows it is coming. To think about death is to think about certainties. If life is filled, or seems filled, with uncertainty, thinking about death is disconcerting. One is reminded of all the plans that have gone astray, about all the dreams that are unfulfilled and not likely to be fulfilled, about the education wasted or unused, about the disorder and disharmony of much family living, about the political and social chaos of the neighborhoods in which we live. We set aside the question of death by saying, "All life is uncertain."

3. *An Interest in Death Is Thought of as an Old Person's Interest*

We associate death with old age, forgetting about its ever-presence for people of all ages in hospitals, on highways, in airplanes, on the streets.

"I am too young to think about it" says it all. Young people and middle-aged people set the considerations of death off till a later time. "I'm not going to die," therefore, "I shall postpone thinking about it." We imagine that older people are preoccupied with thoughts about their own demise, forgetting that they, too, generally speaking, are focusing on the events of life. The picture of the oldtimer on his deathbed, calling for The Book so he can make his religious amends before it is too late, is a characteristic one, on stage and in life. We think we have plenty of time. When we're older, we'll think about it.

People avoid making wills for the same reason. To think about wills is to think about one's own death and about the death of one's loved ones. "I have very little, anyway," says the reluctant consumer, putting it off.

4. *There Is a Lack of Information about the Funeral Field*

Consumers resist change because they lack an understanding of what is happening in the funeral field. Ignorant, we presume high expense is essential. It doesn't happen too often, anyway, so why fuss? Unchallenging, we presume the bill presented is the bill that ought to be. Consumers assume, unless they know to the contrary, that the funeral director would not take advantage of the consumer. It is a common consumer fallacy, based on our need and desire to trust others. We find it difficult to think ill of businessmen.

Conscious-consumer information is scanty in the field. People are reluctant to comparison-shop for a funeral; there seems to be no time when the person is dead and funeral arrangements need to be made.

People do not know even the few laws protecting consumers. When a funeral director says, as many will say, "Embalming is required by law," the consumer rarely returns with the information that embalming is *not* required by law.

Further, few people understand just what a funeral director does. All they know, after he has said, "Don't worry, Mother, we'll take care of everything," is that Dad's body appears in a box in a church-like chapel. What he has done for us, in preparing the body for burial, we once knew intimately and did ourselves. Today's generations, as part of their conscious evasion of death, are pleased to let Mr. George, the funeral director, do it. We'd rather not know, thank you.

5. *Change is Difficult because of the Impact of Guilt*

When we think about all the money we spent at the last funeral (like the money we spent at our daughter's wedding), we are reassured. Money spent relieves guilt. We are relieved about inadequacies in our relationship with the deceased. If we didn't visit Uncle Harry very much in his last years, or if we sort of ignored Mother, if Dad worked a helluva lot and we were never thankful . . . all of these feelings are eased by the knowledge that we did not stint one little bit when it came to funeral expenses. In these situations everyone carries some guilt about with him as baggage.

Under the last-minute pressures of funeral decision-making, people don't always *consciously* say to themselves, "I will feel bad all my life if the funeral isn't adequate," but that is nevertheless what the mood is. If the buyer selects a lower-cost coffin, or holds back on flower arrangements, or resists the rental of many limousines, or in any way backs away from the traditional and known experiences of handling death, he can't change his mind later. Once done, it's done. That pressure, within the buyer's head, sells merchandise.

6. *It's Very Hard to Think Creatively if Worry about What the Neighbors and Friends Will Think Plays a Part in Our Buying Decisions*

If we believe that people will think we're "cheap" if we hold back on expenses, we are willing even to borrow money to make good on the unspoken promises we make to our neighbors to uphold their expectations. Keeping-up-with-the-Joneses is a fact. And it works in all economic classes in our society.

At the conclusions of funeral events, we wait patiently for the approving comments from old friends. "He looked so nice. So much at peace." "The flowers are so beautiful." And eyes reach each other, avoiding the sadness and the impulse to cry, to express, "Everything was done so nicely." "Isn't Mr. Wiggins [the funeral director] so helpful?" The body and the merchandise were delivered in good shape. That is all we want to hear. Our neighbors and friends were pleased.

7. *Cosmic Uncertainties Play a Part, Too*

Suppose it's true that embalmed bodies are recalled by divine powers to live another life in those old shells? And our assumption, defying logic, made it right to keep the body whole and in its original condition, underground? Would our faithlessness (if we cremated the body, or gave it to science) be punished later if we didn't keep the bodies intact for that Divine Recall?

If it is true we return to our Maker, do we know for sure that our return is in spirit alone? Won't the blessed body we stayed with so long go with us? Not knowing carries its burden: without certainty we hedge against it by embalming, by cosmetic work, by surrounding coffins with concrete vaults so that the coffin and its contents won't decay so rapidly.

Older religions, with their heavens and hells, have etched photographic images in our minds. Artists' renderings of tortured spirits are always in human form. We don't want *that* experience; but surely and subtly our minds assume full bodily descent to hell or full bodily ascent upward (the way Jesus went).

Our intellectual rejection of these once-verities may be rewarded, we fear, by heaven or hell. We can't be sure. A residual Sunday school memory emerges at funeral-buying time—and the Judgment Day finality and funereal atmosphere of the funeral home only help the mood to prevail. One might well imagine the average funeral director as a kind of St. Peter, accepting or rejecting prospective guests, making those vital decisions, somberly, firmly.

8. *There Is a Lurking Suspicion that to Entertain Ideas of Change Is to Harbor Subversive Thoughts*

We might be supporting subversive ideas unintentionally. Who wants to be called "un-American" by funeral directors, or by anyone else? The fear of being different is nurtured by many funeral directors themselves, who have pictured advocates of change as Messengers from Moscow or perhaps Peking. Our own love of country means that the funeral director can say to us—and he probably means it—that the business in which he is engaged is tied (with a truly golden thread) to America. And when "God Bless America" is sung at funeral directors' conventions, it means an America that has provided such a good living, without challenge from government, without meaningful alternatives; an America that welcomes an unrestricted private enterprise; an America that praises the successful businessman; an America not yet sure that the consumer has rights and still willing to let him/her depend, by and large, on the mercy of the business community.

9. *"You're an Atheist!"*

Despite an undertow of intellectual honesty in the community that occasionally permits an otherwise-quiet citizen to mutter to a few chosen friends that he is really an atheist, few people are willing to be squelched as such in discussion.

Theism is an acceptable cloak. That religion can and does exist without theism isn't the point. Few people, with or without a higher-value system as a crux in personal decision-making, will fail to cringe at the charge of atheism. It has communist implications, un-American implications. It suggests we don't love our observant parents and grandparents and that we have been cruel enough to reject the religions learned at our parents' knees. It means that we have set up ourselves as enemies of friendly Father Murphy, of gentle Rabbi Goldberg, of everyone who was ever a Believer. It is just too much.

It is no wonder that much commercial activity is handled in red-white-and-blue packaging, with a touch of the divine and eternal in it: the combination is unbeatable. "God Bless Free Enterprise, System Divine . . . ," the college radical's spoof-song of "God Bless America," is not funny to the businessman. He means Business. God has been good to me, says the pious businessman, referring to his material gains. That God hasn't been equally good to those who provided him with the material gains is not an acceptable flip-flop of arguments.

God, perhaps, has even provided the businessman as a kind of intermediary. When we are good and kind to the businessman, offering him our weekly salary-offerings, we are being good to God. No one, perhaps, wishes to operate without divine sanctions. All sides (note our wars) seem to carry with them "God's blessings."

No wonder that the funeral critic is called names. Despite the kids' saying that only sticks and stones hurt, words hurt too. Our buyer resistance and our consumer philosophy are not so strong that we can live with accusations. How do you fight a rumor?

Probing Their Resistance

One would suppose that, in the characteristic American way, funeral businesses would have picked up the harshest criticisms, modified their practices and moved on to greater successes. They could hire, as other businesses do, consumer specialists, to explain consumers to themselves, and themselves to consumers. But that hasn't been the way.

They have remained largely untouched by outside critics, suspicious still of genuine concern, unmodified by government restriction, holding their funereal fortresses from the onslaughts of the enemy.

There are many reasons why the Funeral Establishment resists change:

1. It is a good business, where a man can make his way without too much fear of competition. (There are very few female funeral directors.) The earnings are good and there's lifetime security. His wife and children can expect only comforts.

2. The funeral director is often a leader in his church and community. He is respected by the community's people, who know vaguely what he does, specifically how needed he is. He may contribute heavily to his religious group, thus forestalling much criticism from that sector. Few businessmen have such respect from their church communities. It is almost as if the funeral director were a kind of subclergy, performing vital church functions. That self-image is important to the funeral director, satisfying to his ego, providing psychic rewards available to few.

3. His trade associations call him a "professional," a higher rank than businessman. Thus, in his own mind, he is part of a professional community, an associate of doctors, lawyers and clergymen. That his education as funeral director is minimal and largely technical is ignored. He thinks of himself as a professional: that is enough. His eagerness for connections with other professions suggests his insecurity. Now, seeking links with psychologists, he is trying on "grief therapist" for size. Whether it will fit or not depends largely on how the speculation is received by professionals and consumers alike.

4. The mystique about the American capitalist self-made man is

reassuring for the funeral director. He may even see himself as the last link with the American past of unthreatened and unbridled business-men. A man deserves what he earns, he might well feel, as he sells all he can sell to the unsuspecting and grieving visitor. His prices are his own to keep or expand; his services the same. His business is his business. There is this sense of the capitalist pioneer at work in this field, which is hard for *most* businessmen to know, as the growing consumer awareness and government watchdog activity take their (to us) desired toll.

The funeral director, associating his business with the American Way, may feel he is the last bulwark against communism. That his business is uncontrolled, free from the raging processes of democratic control, assists that impression. Not noticeable in the political com-munity as an advocate of social change (perhaps not noticeable at all, from any viewpoint, as he wends his way among the bodies of all kinds of political people), the funeral director sees his financial destiny as America's. It is natural and understandable. Not quite a crusader, not quite the white-suited warrior on a white horse (well, black on black), the funeral director through his advocacy of "The American Funeral" will keep America on the right track.

5. The air of mystery about the whole funeral business for most people appeals to his own sense of conspiracy, of specialness. If a man does what few others do, if he knows what few others know, if he is, on top of it, a respected citizen, who can complain? To the man who works in an air of mystery, in the dark and unknown recesses of his parlor, will go the credit for being the last man to be subdued if not controlled by consumers. His is not an open business, open to the potshots of the wary, open to the wisdom of the conscious consumer. His cards are close to his black vest.

Shall We Overcome?

The urgent problem rests with us. If it is indeed true that few changes will come about in that industry (or in any industry, for that matter) until consumers know their needs and wants better and act accordingly, it is then true that the consumer seeking enlightenment first must work his way through his own head-problems, find a truer course than the one he has been following and begin to demand and perhaps himself create and build new approaches.

The individual isolated consumer feels drowned, unable to cope with the waves and wash of the marketplace. Even when enlightened, he feels it to be a too difficult task for himself to create changes. Not everyone is a crusader. He needs others. He knows he needs others. *That is a beginning.*

To review the reasons for resistance is to agree with them. "Yes, that's right." "Oh, that's so true." But something is lacking.

The lack is the will to organize.

Simple organization does something no single consumer can do. It provides backbone, a framework in which individuals can nudge each other to change. That is the basic argument of this book: Individuals alone can do little, but concerned people, working together in a democratic and caring spirit, can produce changes in themselves and in their communities.

There are cranky individual consumers. They make their way alone. Social salvation (or social justice) calls for more than a clear-thinking individual. Bands of clear-thinking individuals are needed. Social solutions are required.

It is unlikely that a private-profit-oriented system will voluntarily change. It is providing, and that is what their more articulate spokesmen tell you clearly, what consumers want.

They are right, these graduates of Columbaria University, the key is in the mind of the consumer. They are providing what we want. So we shall have to *want* differently.

One Group Tries the Hardest Way of All

One can want new approaches; it is another thing actually to *do* them.

The radical logic of the discussion would lead us into the practice of burying our own dead.

But that's not necessary, most of us would exclaim. Besides, it's too uncomfortable a thought. Few people are willing to take on the task of washing bodies, of preparing them for a ceremonial wake or for ultimate disposition.

However, one group in Yellow Springs, Ohio, faced up to the challenge. Ernest Morgan, in the fifth edition of *A Manual of Simple Burial*,[1] shows another way.

A committee [of the Friends Meeting] was formed in 1948. Unable to find a precedent, it studied burial law and found that religious organizations might care for their own dead. It polled the Meeting membership and found overwhelming preference for cremation, and for dealing directly with death, rather than through morticians. In recent years there has been increasing preference for bequeathal to a medical school.

Committee members visited health officers of the state and county to get their understanding and cooperation. The cooperation of a crematory was secured. Simplicity and spiritual values were stressed. Discussions and studies continued for several years until the thinking of the membership and the knowledge of the committee reached the point of action.

Most of the Meeting families are registered with the committee. One form is used, including a "Registration of Intent," authorizing the committee to act and stating what arrangements are desired, the needed legal and biographical data, space for endorsement by next of kin, and names of relatives to be notified. This form must be filled out in advance. A contribution of $5 or $10 is expected from each family registered.

At time of death, or when death is expected, the first action is to give the family support in whatever ways may be needed. Help with the children or with food, a lift with the housework, hospitality for visiting relatives—a rallying of friends in a quiet coordinated way. This is done by the Meeting, not just by the committee.

Immediately on death a committee member takes the death certificate to the county health office and gets a transit permit. The next of kin endorses the Registration of Intent and signs an authorization to cremate. (He also gives the committee a check made out to the crematory for the cost of cremation. Later he pays for the box plus legal fees and incidentals. No personal services are paid for, and the total expense is usually under $100.)

If, for any reason, a body must be held more than a day (except in winter weather) before cremation or burial, embalming or refrigeration are needed, or the body may be placed in a hermetically sealed bag.

The time and place of a memorial meeting are decided, generally three or four days after death. Friends and relatives are notified and an obituary is given to the newspapers. Apart from consulting on the general plan of the memorial meeting, the family is not called upon to make any decisions at the time of death.

The committee gets from its storage a plain plywood box of suitable size, places the body in it, loads it into a station wagon and delivers it to the crematory or the medical school, where a receipt is obtained. The metal handles are removed from the box and taken back for future use. In the case of cremation the ashes may be called for in a day or so, or may be sent by mail.

That's not our cup of tea, most consumers will say. It's too hard, too big a leap into unknown experience. It took years for that Meeting to reach that point, and it would take years for any other group even to consider moving in that direction. We can only uphold it as an ideal, something for tomorrow.

Our lifelong preparation for funerals, or rather our lack of it, probably requires the funeral director as we know him, the setting in which he works, the cemetery as we see it in our mind.

Changes will occur, of course, and we may not even recall their beginnings. We forget that Social Security was once a Socialist platform plank, that supermarkets and shopping centers didn't exist, that doctors used to visit our homes, that dentists worked without anesthetics, that a bread and cake truck used to visit our neighborhood, that milk was delivered almost universally to our doors, that insurance men collected 10 cents a week at the door, that beer was bought by the growler (to take home for Dad and his visiting friends), that butter was cut out of a wooden tub in the grocery store, that milk and sour cream were ladled out at the counter, that the horse was the mighty kingpin of our transportation system.

In the Meantime . . . Harbingers of Change

Not all consumers have stood by mutely, watching the dollars go by. In fact, a half-million people in the United States have broken the chain of silence and announced, through their membership in new kinds of organizations, that they want to have a say in the disposition of their own bodies.

Their basic position in organizing and joining what are called memorial societies is that, by joining together, they will try to get what they want: simpler, less expensive funerals. They do this by planning their own funerals ahead of time and, in many cases, by securing the support of funeral directors willing to cooperate with the societies.

The more people gaze directly in this way at the face of death, the greater the possibility of change. Memorial societies are a major reflection of the new consumer consciousness.

It All Begins with a Memorial Society

3

When strangers first see the literature of a memorial society, they are confused.

One college administrator, looking cursorily at the literature of a memorial society organized by students, thought that it had to do with honoring deceased or retired faculty members; another, in the same college's public relations office, thought it was a clever private business scheme designed to offer cutrate funerals to members.

The literature of the movement is often austere. It's not prone to catchy titles, or emotion-grabbing headlines. However, half a million Americans have overcome the sparseness actually to read the words, sign forms, fill out a small check and become members.

There must be something to it.

There is.

The memorial society is a healthy consumer response to the funeral marketplace. A member-owned and controlled organization, the memorial society advocates advance planning and low-cost funerals. As an idea, it is the main repository of consumer protest in the United States at the present time, the main thrust for positive alternatives to exploitation by the funeral industry.

There are practical services, too.

Why Organize a Memorial Society?

The motives of organizers of memorial societies have varied, as people vary. Uniting them has been a passion for alternatives.

Some have been furious at maltreatment, rudeness or insensitivity. The funeral director, with the body in his back room, has control. Unwanted unctuousness, cloaking his firm intentions to spend his client's money, aggravates many a soul.

The justification of expenses by resort to nonexistent laws has aroused anger among many. Unaware at the time, the victim later feels the slow burn. Embalming is not required by law, yet the expense was incurred. Thousands upon thousands of embalmings have been performed as a result of that pretense. One funeral director in Rockland County, New York, had the wife's body embalmed before the deceased's husband had even returned home from a distant city, before even preliminary discussions had been held. That her body was to be cremated made the director's presumptuousness even more absurd.

Few religious institutions and few funeral directors have done much for the idea of cremation, leading some organizers to create societies to encourage freedom and self-help in that direction. A growing public consciousness and the altered opinion of some churches have contributed to a new willingness to explore this approach, with symbolic distribution of the ashes over loved garden spots, "to the four winds," at sea.

Some organizers enter the field for profoundly philosophical or religious reasons. Feeling that the disposal of the body, its display, a ceremony around the casket and similar practices make the object of a funeral ceremony the dead body, such people have argued that the *life* of the person is the proper focus. The elaborate funereal surroundings of the average funeral home, the black-and-maroonness of the decor, the hushed voices, the thick carpeting, these people insist, emphasize death. Many prefer the quick disposition of the body, bypassing any use whatsoever of the funeral parlor, and emphasize in the place of the funereal occasion the life-emphasis of the typical memorial meeting.

Some local groups have been initiated by people, offended by contemporary American funeral practices, who argue that what happens to the body is unimportant. Simply dispose of it! Focus on life! A few resist ceremony of any kind, opposing for themselves whose destinies they can after all control, what they consider to be the false religiosity of modern practices. "When I'm dead, who cares?" might be the question. "Put me away fast and worry about something else." "It's just a time for a minister or a rabbi and a funeral director to make a buck; it's not worth it."

Historically, memorial societies have offered members information on alternatives to the conventional funeral. Planning forms enable decisions—such as the donation of the body to science, the contribution of vital organs to those needing them, eye transplants—to be made well in advance of death.

Some intensely practical people, consumer-conscious persons, have functioned from a strictly economic view. Funerals, they argue, are a waste of money. If money must be spent, give it as a memorial gift, in the name of the dead person, to a cause that meant something to the dead person. Money is better spent on the living. Some say lavish spending on a funeral is immoral.

So the range of human reaction is wide.

The passion for alternatives, so clearly a unifying factor among all these people, has been compounded by a sense of how little one person can do alone. How do you change a practice that is so ingrained in people that they feel bad if they don't go through with it? How do you change an industry gone awry, with such powerful lobbies, concerned with making money when you are least able to resist spending it? Memorial societies seem to provide an answer, for their members and perhaps for a nation looking for alternatives.

These reformers are ordinary citizens and good Americans. Drawing on the self-help and mutual-aid characteristics of historic America, they have found answers to problems facing them. Creating voluntary organizations, served by unpaid leaders, democratic in spirit and content, these leaders have pioneered in the best American spirit.

These people possess the craggy-jawed kind of rugged individualism that sticks with the issue until it is resolved. They are not afraid of restrictive legislation nor of threats from the bulldozing lobbyists for the rich and powerful. They continue despite the sarcasms of the unregenerate anti-intellectuals and the blandishments of liberals who seem to be with you. They are the ones who have, as their neighbors might put it, "gone crazy" and decided to do something about funerals.

What Do Memorial Societies Do?

The most valuable contribution made by memorial societies to their members is in the encouragement of advance planning which is the key to sanity in the funeral field. When death comes to Mrs. Smith, Mr. Smith or another person must make the arrangements. Suppose no one knows Mrs. Smith's own desires? What happens then? Money becomes no object. Driven by sentiment, by those natural feelings of grief and guilt, Mr. Smith may buy more than he and Mrs. Smith would ever have considered at a calmer time. To repeat: no other purchase is made in the marketplace under such extraordinary pressures.

The funeral director, through a few probing questions, is skillfully able to detect a lack of planning. He also senses the financial capability of the family. He assures the survivor that "everything will be taken care of." And the family member, still finding it hard to believe that he is in the midst of planning a funeral for one who was alive and happy and breathing just yesterday, is led to a display room, or one of several (if they are arranged by general price categories) to make a selection. It is coarse, the survivor is likely to feel, to be concerned about money "at a time like this."

So much for the sad sales routine. Too many have experienced it. What would planning do about this?

If Mr. and Mrs. Smith had set aside time in their undoubtedly busy lives, he would be functioning as her agent in his visit to the funeral director. Mrs. Smith, you might say, is leaning on his arm, is with him. He is there to carry out Mrs. Smith's wishes. The armor of planning strengthens sales resistance. Mr. Smith would not be a free person, free to make his own decisions. His love for Mrs. Smith, his caring about her desires, would lead him to insist, if such was the plan, that the simplest pine coffin ($64 to $95) would be more than ample; that there will be no need for embalming; since no display of the body is desired, there is no need for cosmetic work. Similarly, there is no need for elaborate dressing of the body. There will be, if that is what they had planned, a quiet gathering of friends about the coffin that evening, followed by the funeral director's station wagon removing the body to the family plot, where no final ceremony is planned.

The variations are numberless. Immediate burial. Immediate cremation. A modest coffin, in the $175 to $250 range. But none of it would have been possible if planning had not occurred.

Planning could also deal with desires for cremation and disposition of ashes, or with donation of bodies to medical science, with eye donations.

The last will and testament, unfortunately, is the private place where many people feel their planning should be recorded. That has been a tragic mistake that memorial societies have tried to correct through constant education. The will, often discovered and read after the body is long gone and buried, may spell out such wishes, but by then it is useless instruction.

Memorial societies provide special forms for planning. (See Appendix A for the basic planning form of the Queens Memorial Society. Many memorial societies also make available an unusual overall planning form, entitled "Putting My House in Order" (see Appendix B).

A planning form, of course, like a will, has no life of its own. It does not miraculously appear at the time of death, with red lights flashing, and announce that the deceased had desires. Were a single copy of the form to be filled out and filed among private papers, it would have the usefulness of will arrangements: too late.

Memorial societies offer several copies of the planning form. The message is stated and obvious. When you have completed the form, send a copy to your memorial society, to the next of kin, your minister, your lawyer. Whomever. The point is: don't keep it a secret. People will have to make decisions after you have gone. If you want to exercise choice, this is the time.

The most sophisticated use of the planning form is to let it create an occasion for serious thought by the family. Here it is. This is a form. Before we can fill it out, we have to talk about it. Let's discuss it, tonight, after supper. There is no doubt that many members of memorial societies, despite their advanced consciousness, have tucked away the papers for another time. Or the papers have been completed but not shared with relatives and key people.

Perhaps the feeling is that it's like signing your own death certificate. Yet many people report the sense of relief after having completed the forms: a long-delayed task has been completed. The feeling is often the same when a will has been signed and tucked away: decisions have been made. Of course the planning form can be changed, just as the will can be changed.

Why Have Organizations Ignored the Need for Funeral Planning?

It is strange that churches and synagogues and Friends Meetings and ashrams, concerned as they are with life values and life questions, do not emphasize (if not require) funeral planning among their members. They, too, would rather not raise the questions. The mystique surrounding the funeral industry, the awe, the fearsomeness of thinking about death have captured them. The professional clergy are available at time of death, but few see it as their job to be available when thought about death is going on, much less to encourage the planning process itself. (Christians might well ponder the significance of Jesus' planning his own death, which he felt was inevitable. He was ready for it, we are told, as he decided to return to the big city.)

Those cooperatives that go beyond merely conducting business and emphasize cooperation as a way of life and those communes and intentional communities that dot the countryside fail, too, when they ignore planning for death. Given the professions of life-oriented groups, they perform an actual disservice to their members when they leave the burden of death arrangements to relatives and friends who must proceed into the funeral marketplace unprepared, unwarned, unaware of the desires of the deceased.

The most radical group in the United States, the pacifist Movement for a New Society (MNS)[1]—a handful with a vision—is likely to exercise more influence for good than most other groups seeking social change because, unlike most radicals, who live compartmentalized lives, the MNS people believe they can be more effective by experimenting with a lifestyle that integrates the elements of existence. They have combined the teaching/learning necessities, the public demonstrations, the wisdom of cooperative living, the serious thought and analysis, pamphlet-publishing in one movement. In theory, the group (centered at the Philadelphia Life Center but with links with comparable groups elsewhere) encompasses a birth-to-death view, an overall view. But they have failed thus far, despite the efforts of concerned outsiders to urge them otherwise, to give systematic thought to death-planning. They have a Clearness Committee to interview potential participants who want to be *in* the group; what happens to those who *leave* through death has been ignored.

Women's Liberation, the most significant person-reevaluation movement of our times, focuses on the discovery and rediscovery of the person. A woman has the right to use her body in the way she wishes! It is her body. It is her life. She is not a slave. Yet, few if any of those revolutionaries—those seeking strong and substantial social change—have uttered the key words: to be concerned about life is to have control, too, over the way the body is disposed of at death. Men's Liberation, that little splinter movement (with the hardest job of all) is miserably lacking in social philosophy. It has no concern with death-planning. The few remaining flower children, the civil rights activists, the organized welfare poor, the New Left (the Old Left is ornately conventional)—all have failed to consider the question. No one, it appears, is going to die. We are all going to live forever.

Other movements and value systems having failed, it is possible that a vigorous and unrelenting consumer consciousness may at last be the instrument to help us break through our traditional hesitations. There are certainly a few people who harbor superstitions and are consequently fearful of discussing death, but they are too few to concern us. The great majority of people, unwilling for all the good reasons we give ourselves to face up to their own deaths, fall into the trap laid by funeral directors who have thrived because of our problem with death. Cost consciousness, a new wisdom about the proper uses of money, greater evaluation of personal lifestyles, new awareness of creative uses of dollar-power, a resistance to exploitation (Enough is enough!) may provide the key that has been missing: purely temporal concerns, purely dollars-and-cents perspectives may do more to help us evaluate our life-and-death styles than all the high-minded idea systems we have inherited from the past.

Planning Preserves Choice

The capitalist marketplace has always emphasized freedom of choice. Unfortunately, that has not always meant a choice between equally good and effective alternatives. It is often between good and bad. If we are "taken," it's our fault, we chose incorrectly. It is a troublesome philosophy.

The funeral parlor's psychology is geared to what directors call a traditional American funeral. This funeral is the one they are best prepared to provide and it is the one that provides them with the most money.

The act of planning emphasizes the right to choose. It permits the consumer to choose which of the services provided by a funeral director he may wish and which he chooses to reject. It may also mean that he will decide to use only the funeral director's station wagon to cart the body to a nearby medical institution for research purposes.

A Close Look at Choices

Assuming that the wise consumer's concern is with relative simplicity and with low cost, there is a wide variety of options available. They should be looked at in some detail.

The consumer may choose to go the conventional American Funeral route, but choose to do it simply. A plain wooden coffin may be selected. If a last look at the body is desired, it can be cosmetically reorganized with a single evening's viewing by close relatives and friends held at the funeral parlor. (But watch those mounting costs!) Or, if body viewing is not desired, the request can be for a closed coffin, with enough seats for visitors to gather for a modest program, with brief recollections. A modest display of flowers may be chosen or none at all. There can be music. At the end of the evening, the coffin, with its enclosed body, can be taken out of the "reposing room" and stored for early-morning delivery to the cemetery.

Cemetery occasions are a choice, too. The consumer may wish a simple affair, with a few spoken words, while the immediate family and close friends stand by as the coffin is lowered and the grave filled with the waiting dirt.

Or the route can lead to the crematory after the funeral parlor ceremony. That visit can often include a simple ceremony, too, a brief recollection of the life of the deceased, preceding the removal of the coffin and the body to the furnace. Many people associated with religious institutions will resist the invitations offered by funeral parlors to use their churchlike chapels and reposing rooms and will insist that the church provide the setting for the religious service. The funeral director will prepare the body and provide the coffin and the transportation, but the church and the clergy, in these cases, will play a role that has been slipping away from them as the funeral industry grows in power and authority. Many church people have come to resent the casual assumption made by many funeral directors that their establishments are the proper places for funerals.

These are the simplest uses of the funeral parlor's services and are likely to be the plan of those consumers who find it most difficult to break away from cultural and familial patterns but who nevertheless seek to avoid the overdone and overblown occasion one associates with the American funeral.

Supposing that the consumer has another idea of "American" and wishes to conserve resources, he might proceed to other choices.

Immediate burial is a first possibility. The funeral parlor can be directed to pick up the body from the hospital or home, place it in a simple coffin and take it directly to a cemetery, where friends and relatives may gather for reflection, prayers or just quiet observance of the proceedings.

Immediate cremation is a second possibility. The process may be the same.

The choices are many and so are the pitfalls. The buyer, if he is troubled by the insistence of the funeral director that embalming and other purchases (like underground vaults to enclose the coffin . . . a coffin for the coffin) are somehow required, can resort to the simple mechanism of requesting the use of the telephone to call the local health department. An independent call may also be made to the cemetery itself, to inquire if in fact it does require a vault for the coffin.

Sometimes, the mere suggestion by the consumer that he* knows what he wants and that he has a right to his choice may be enough to cool the sales ardor of the director. There is of course the ultimate threat of taking the business elsewhere, a rare action but one which should be inspired by the new consumer consciousness. The consumer has a right to choice, as he has to his money's worth. He should not be led into unwanted purchases of services of any kind against his wish, and it certainly should not be under the pressure of nonexistent "law." Students in one eastern college, sent by their instructor to talk with funeral directors about their prices and practices, sometimes received the impression that directors make up the laws as they go along.

Informed consumers, firmly insistent on what they want, can have their way. Too, it is helpful to recall and use the oft-stated funeral director's view that his desire is to meet the wishes of the family; insist, then, that their wishes be followed. A firm stride, a proud independence, a right to choice will not be overcome by the blandishments of a sales-oriented and insensitive funeral director. Not all funeral directors respond positively to people who seem to have plans in hand. But advise your expected survivors, in your planning form, clearly and concisely what you wish. That action will often firm up the backbones of grieving survivors.

Not all people wish to focus on the bodies of the deceased. The person planning his own funeral may have participated in open and closed casket events and found them wanting. Too much attention is placed on the body of the person in those circumstances. Immediate burial and immediate cremation, in which the body is removed from living scenes rapidly, may be his wish, with no graveside meeting. But there are ways to emphasize life.

The Memorial Meeting

The memorial meeting, held in a few days or even weeks after death, is a time when survivors can meet to console each other, to

*The use of the masculine gender to mean both sexes is increasingly a problem for women and men sensitive to the psychology of language. Unfortunately, no new words have as yet arisen which would solve the problem gracefully. Hopefully, the new awareness will create new forms.

comfort relatives, to talk with each other about the life and works of their departed common friend.

A story I wrote for the November-December 1971 issue of *Co-op Information,* a publication of the Cooperative League of the USA,[2] tells the story of one such memorial meeting. Reflecting as it does the high emotion of such an occasion for a dead friend, it portrays the effective spirit that is possible. It's a rare American funeral that catches this mood.

ROBERT L. SMITH *1912–1971*
REFLECTIONS ON A CO-OP LEADER WHO WILL BE MISSED

"Did you hear Bob Smith died . . . ?" I had just returned from a trip and the message, in its coldness, grabbed me.

Bob Smith died on June 23, 1971. Born in the year 1912 in Woodside, New York, married to Jacqueline, father of Jennifer and Roger. Resident of Pelham, New York. Employee of Consumers Union. Long associated with cooperatives. One-time member of the Cooperative League board.

Cold statistics rarely comprehend a man. They evoke neither justice nor the wide-ranging love of which we are capable. A man has died. His works are behind him.

A man's friends are the final repository of what he was. The ashes don't matter. Our eternity rests in the hearts and minds of those who remember, who shared, for an instant or part of a generation, that strange phenomenon, life.

A gathering in New York City in late July brought 80 friends together, to recall the spirit of a life, its ups and downs and adventures, its great moments and little touches.

Yes, there was history there. Bob had touched the reform movements of our day and had been a part of them. Patterns emerged as people spoke. One man united, for a brief moment in time, eighty people. Bob had been in his life and was in his death a hub for large wheels of association.

A distinguished professor from Massachusetts recalled the operations of a co-op gas station in student days. "Learning by doing," he called it. A Philadelphia lawyer recalled a Pendle Hill conference on co-ops and "Bob's concern for what is better." Another spoke of 40 years of association.

Bob's management of New Haven's co-op supermarkets, a trip to Antigonish, service as educator-organizer in the Eastern Cooperative League and the Palo Alto co-op, a study tour of co-ops in Europe, his latter years with the Consumers Union of the U.S., his role in today's consumer movement were the stuff of Bob's connections with people.

After World War II, he travelled in Europe for 3 months for the Co-op Freedom Fund, helping in the urgent recovery of European co-ops. His strong Co-op background led in 1957 to a 3-month trip to co-ops in Great Britain as special representative of the U.S. Department of Labor. He gave long service to the Cooperative League Board. Bob was a prime mover in the Consumer Federation of America. And, through it all, over the years, he was modest, eager only for the causes named and not his own.

There were laughter over funny incidents and moments of high sharing. There was quiet reflection when people spoke of his strong loyalties, his concern for family, his "building of a personality." A neighbor spoke of the "loving emanations" from the Smith home in Pelham. Bob never became angry; he chuckled at man's infinite variations of perfidy, balancing his deep compassion for people with a sense of what is possible.

Slides, playing on a back wall, were a continuing reminder of the man. Witnesses at the meeting could turn away for a brief moment from the outpouring of affection to see Bob at a camping site, in front of a co-op somewhere, smiling with friends and family, enjoying his Vermont hilltop.

Jackie Smith, Bob's wife and associate over the years, alternately smiling at old recollections and reflecting quietly on forgotten incidents, concluded the meeting with cherished quotations from Walt Whitman.

Her reading finished, we grasped each other's hands and stood together. The strains of Sibelius' Finlandia took the place of words and we were quiet.

I walked tall when I left the meeting. I had met Bob's friends. I had met Bob. Eighty lives and more had been moved.

Ashes

Because of the typical stress and financial burdens we link with earth burial, many people have turned to cremation of the body to provide meaningful ceremony. Unless the funeral director has sold the consumer a permanent niche in a columbarium for the ashes, the body's ashes can be distributed among the places and scenes associated with life. Those who have moved in this direction think of it as an incredibly beautiful and sensitive moment, when the scattered ashes find their place in the ocean, on a loved mountainside or among flowers and bushes tended so carefully in life.

Earth burial, as it is conducted now, with sealed coffins and vaults designed to perpetuate the false image that the body stays in its original condition, does not provide that sense of spiritual connection, of a life joining Life, of returning to the soil from whence we all came.

"Ashes to ashes, dust to dust," and a winsome sense of fatalism we associate with those words are denied us by current earth-burial practices. If we could only be buried wrapped in a simple shroud . . . connecting closely with the earth . . . we would have an alternative.

Body Donation

No act of burial, no act of cremation seems as direct a contribution to the surviving world as that of body donation and the related gift of various critically needed parts of the body.

When bodies are donated to schools of anatomy, they become available for the countless studies necessary for medicine's advance. The donations of organs play an exciting role—in a direct sense—for the ultimate beneficiary is not merely the general advance of mankind through better-trained and more highly skilled doctors but an actual individual who receives the needed body parts.

The most dramatic and perhaps best known and widely accepted is the corneal transplant. The generous thought requires planning, for within a few hours after death the vital part must be lifted from the eye, transported to its new location and transplanted before the cells wither. Eye Banks[3] exist in various parts of the country, and thousands of individuals carry identification cards from those banks informing those who find them that the eyes of the card-bearer are intended for use by the Eye Bank. What a gift! making it possible for someone else to see! It is a sad commentary on our times that there are people waiting for the gift of sight, while millions of people die without even knowing, perhaps even caring, that their eyes can live after them.

Ernest Morgan, quoted earlier, a pioneer in the funeral-planning field and a founding member of the Continental Association of Funeral and Memorial Societies,[4] offers in his *A Manual of Death Education and Simple Burial* (6th edition) an entire section called, "How the Dead Can Help the Living." In it, he describes twelve ways:

1. Permit an autopsy, which can be helpful in "improving the knowledge and experience of doctors."
2. Bequeath the body to a medical school, aiding in the training of future doctors and dentists.

3. Bequeath the eyes to an Eye Bank, making corneal transplants available to those who need new corneas to see once again.
4. Bequeath the ear bones to a Temporal Bone Bank, especially the ear bones of those with hearing problems, aiding research in that field.
5. Bequeath kidneys, to replace diseased tissue with new.
6. Encourage radiation research, which, by studying the bodies of disease-free young people, increases understanding of the amount of radiation in our bodies.
7. Contribute pituitary glands, whose extract is helpful to those children with deficiencies.
8. Participate in the Living Bank, which coordinates "the disposition and use of anatomical gifts."
9. Contribute to the Naval Medical Research Center, whose Tissue Bank accepts donations, particularly from the under-35 age group.
10. Donate skin for dressing and grafting, to aid those with serious burns.
11. Donate blood, which, taken from cadavers, helps those needing transfusions of new blood.
12. Recycle non-organic materials, such as eyeglasses, pills and tooth fillings.

Barring the development of a community in which, for reasons of societal survival, individuals would have no choice in the matter, the decision to participate in these life-giving enterprises now requires the conscious act of the donor, who, while alive, promises to make his body or portions of his body available to others. Given the urgent needs for such voluntary giving, there is every argument for an acceleration of planning among thoughtful people.

Illusions of Planning

Trade unions and fraternal orders with death benefits (dollar amounts available to survivors to help pay for funerals, and discount arrangements with funeral parlors), the custom of buying family plots, as well as the personal-life-insurance program with the sole function of paying for funeral expenses ("I don't want to be a burden on the kids" is the rationale) have unfortunately fostered an illusion of planning. Few trade unions and fraternal orders have used their considerable buying power to reduce funeral costs, which might leave more money for survivors. In the matter of death benefits, the costs of funerals tend to meet the amount of money available. That's a strange kind of topsy-turvy planning, if we want to ascribe the lofty quality of planning to something like that! It is no wonder, given the sales propensities and profit-needs of the funeral director, that he is likely to inquire first of the death benefits available to the deceased. Adding Social Security benefits, a little judgment on the capacity of the survivors to take on expenses, perhaps a look at their clothing, their educational level, maybe the car they use to come to the funeral parlor, and the funeral director knows just about the amount of money the family might be willing to spend, and he leads them down his cushy rugs to financial excess.

The karate chop of the conscious consumer who says he knows what he wants and tells his potential survivors so is the *plan*. Without it, without the planning effort, the funeral director has every right in our capitalist society to do the best he can to sell as much as he thinks he can. The doctrine of *caveat emptor,* let the buyer beware, is at work until planning occurs; then *caveat venditor,* let the seller beware, becomes the rule. The family with a *plan* has made up its own mind, the seller knows, and he must provide what the family wants. The arguments for planning seem so sensible and so clear that it is strange that *only* five hundred thousand persons are associated with memorial societies. A new consumer consciousness, spreading among millions, will change the picture and will accelerate more consumer control over the total funeral process.

Too many families, smugly satisfied with their costly purchase of a family plot sold them by a persistent salesman, believe they have planned. There's many a dollar to be spent 'twixt the death bed and the final plot; their enthusiasm to rest in good old Grassy View Memorial Knolls, or whatever sounds final and beautiful and death-denying, has blinded them to the biggest expense of all, the costs of the goods and services provided by the middleman, who will escort their bodies to the final resting place.

Cooperating Funeral Directors

Memorial societies, by and large, have felt it helpful to locate funeral directors who will cooperate with their members. Because of the traditional secretiveness and suspicion one finds in the funeral fraternity, this is not a matter of thumbing one's way through the

Yellow Pages and merely making a phone call. But some memorial societies have been able to develop mutual agreements, with assured price lists made available to members.

There aren't many funeral directors in the United States, fewer than twenty-five thousand. Of that number only a small handful cooperate with memorial societies. If there were more memorial societies, serving larger constituencies, more might be invited to participate. Perhaps more funeral directors, if they understood and appreciated the high-minded motives of memorial societies, would be willing to serve persons through those groups.

The experience of the Rockland County (N. Y.) Memorial Society[5] may be typical. Founded in 1964, it had about seventy families in membership for several years. An effort to secure funeral-director cooperation within the county had failed. Finally, it was decided to use the funeral directors serving New York City memorial societies. While this was inconvenient because of distance (the county is a growing suburb of the city), the Society could at least offer the practical services of funeral directors experienced in the handling of funerals for memorial societies.

Some years later the growing Society, with a larger membership, pressed harder for local cooperation. At the request of the Society's members, voiced at an annual meeting, the board of directors sent a letter to every county funeral director listed in the local telephone book. Each was sent a list of prices made available by the more-distant New York City directors and each was cordially invited to participate in the Rockland County group's program. Out of some twenty, three responded. Agreements were reached with two, who are reported to be providing satisfactory service to members, now numbering some four hundred persons.

The following are the services and prices offered by one of the cooperating directors in Rockland County, which compare favorably to rates offered the general public:

Immediate Cremation $230 plus $75
                                                         crematory charges
Includes local removal, health department papers, transfer to crematory, plain pine casket, holding cremated remains for disposition or instructions, personal services.

Immediate Burial $220, plus
                                        cemetery expenses*
 Includes local removal, health department papers, plain pine casket,
 conveyance to local cemetery, personal services.

Cremation with Viewing and Attendance $405, plus $75
                                        crematory charges
 Includes local removal, health department papers, embalming and
 dressing, embossed wood casket, use of chapel for services, transfer by
 hearse to crematory, personal services.

Burial with Viewing and Attendance $460, plus
                                        cemetery expenses
 Includes local removal, health department papers, use of chapel for
 services, embalming and dressing, embossed wood casket, conveyance
 by hearse to local cemetery, personal services.

Delivery to Medical School $75

Note: All transportation charges outside Rockland County, $0.60 per mile
extra.

*Cemetery expenses are a disbursement and are added to costs. Cemetery expenses
vary according to established costs in each individual cemetery.

When the very first distribution of prices of New York City directors to members was made, one member wrote to the Society and said
that she wished she had had the information a week earlier, since she
had just spent $1,000. on a comparable program. These prices are set
against a background of high prices: one director confided to a society
officer that his funerals started at $1,000 and were never less.

Funeral directors could compete with each other. But their professional ethics, determined by themselves, do not permit the advertising
of prices. Competition would lower prices, causing those who fail to
attract customers to drop out. Surviving funeral homes, charging less,
would be volume-operators. At the present time, few funeral parlors
are busy all the time. Many lie dormant for days without activity.
Such waste can be eliminated by a competitive process.

It is surprising that any funeral directors cooperate with memorial
societies. They sense, correctly, that the burden of criticism they have
received has emanated from memorial societies and that most dissent

from the traditional American funerals rests among memorial society members.

Why, then, do they cooperate? The reasons will vary.

1. If word got out that no funeral director would cooperate with well-meaning funeral reformers, it would look bad. This way they defuse the critics a little and get the business, too, though on a modified scale.

2. A few funeral directors are high-minded and ethical persons, who welcome an opportunity to break from the past and reputations of their colleagues. Cooperation with a memorial society in no way diminishes the ability of a director to deal with other consumers in the usual way. Strains of liberalism and fairness have their impact. The occasional funeral director, in this spirit, will accentuate his service motive, emphasizing that people can do whatever they want to do. If they want to go the memorial society way, why, that's their business, not his.

3. Some funeral directors need the business. A new man in the field, perhaps a free-lancer working out of the parlors of others, can use the good will he would receive from successful experiences with members of the community. Good experience—even with a memorial society —sends out positive ripples; the returning waves bring in new business. Word gets around.

4. Even an established funeral practice can use the business, to fill in the idle hours between regular funerals. The property, the staff must be maintained—even while inactive—and good business practice dictates that idle time and property are lost money.

5. A funeral director may want to be his own man, thus reflecting, in a positive way, the rugged individualistic beliefs of his fraternity. He accepts the jibes of his colleagues, patiently explains his position and firmly changes the subject. He's not going to let others, even his business friends, tell him what to do.

6. A handful of directors have built a reputation of interest in the work of memorial societies and have themselves emphasized low-cost funerals and advance planning. It is a natural wedding of interests.

Though the reasons will vary from director to director, the final reality is the same: an agreement or contract is developed between the director and the memorial society, and the memorial society can feel that its members will be spared the "hassle" of negotiation. The words, "I am a member of the memorial society," or, "The deceased was a member of the memorial society," will send clear messages to the director: "This one gets special treatment." Few cooperating funeral directors have violated the trust implicit in the agreements.

As uneasy an alliance as it is, the cooperative relationship provides a valuable service to the members of the memorial society. They are assured that such a funeral director does not need a long philosophical discourse on advance planning and a plea for respect for the wishes of the deceased—particularly at such an awkward time. From the price lists that have been circulated to members, they know that the funeral director is departing from his usual charge.

Basically, the family that is a member of a memorial society controls the negotiations, for it knows what it wants. And the chances are that it will receive what it wants.

Most cooperating funeral directors are willing to maintain a file for a memorial society member, keeping a copy of the "Expression of Wishes." They will welcome a visit, too, from a member desiring to discuss details before filling out such a planning form. These are not unreasonable men. They are not like the cynical businessmen who say, "Bring me the body and then I will discuss prices," a statement which shocked New York City college students on visiting some funeral directors.

There are probably many who would be willing to participate in a responsible cooperating relationship with a memorial society, but there are either no memorial societies in their community (more than likely, since there are few) or the memorial society has decided that it cannot use additional funeral directors until its membership grows.

Dr. Leroy Bowman, addressing the founding meetings of the Consumers Memorial Society[6] in New York, urged the new group to limit the number of funeral directors with whom it would work. He argued that if there are too many directors for a society and not enough business to make much difference to any one of them, they will lose interest in cooperating. The advice makes sense. A form of group buying, an agreement with a funeral director (or two or three) assures better service for members as well as a possibility of more business for the director. Everyone is the gainer, a characteristic of cooperation. In all of New York City there are only a half-dozen cooperating funeral directors. They are enough for the memorial societies as they are now constituted. One or two have worked with memorial societies for years and are deeply interested in the approach; the others are "accommodating."

Good Ideas: Let's Begin!

The organization of a memorial society is relatively simple. It is a service organization. It is an educational organization. It is, above all, a membership organization, a cooperative effort of people who want to help each other plan their own funerals, to find and work with willing funeral directors and to give a boost to the funeral reform idea.

Most memorial societies are small. A few large ones have so much work that needs to be done that they have hired secretaries to manage the mail, call meetings, process the work. But the greater number do as much as the members want to do voluntarily.

All that is necessary to begin such a society is a living-room meeting of people who have expressed an interest in the problem. Your living room will do. We are sometimes hesitant to "start things," but the rewards of such effort are satisfying. Consider the following letter:

Dear Genevieve:

I've been giving a lot of thought to funerals these days. I want to plan my own funeral. I think it's a good idea, and I've been hearing of other people who want to do the same thing.

I don't know any other way than planning to make my own wishes known to my survivors so that I can have the kind of remembrance I want. I'm troubled because not enough people are using their heads on this subject.

Do you think it might be a good idea for some of us to form a memorial society in our area, which would provide planning materials for us and which would encourage other people to plan ahead also? If enough of us get together, we might be able to work out a group arrangement with a local funeral parlor to help keep costs down, too. I thought you might be interested in working on this idea with me and some others. I feel I can't do it alone.

Can you come to my house next Monday night at 7? It will be good to see you.

Cordially,
Adelaide Johnson

Naturally, you'd select the recipients carefully. Some friends might collapse on receiving such a note, unless you know they've thought about forward-looking subjects. One or two people will think you've gone off the deep end, but that's a risk we all take when we start anything new, and it's a special problem in the funeral field.

The first meeting will be a bit awkward. Unless you know to the contrary, you might just as well assume that most of your friends have rarely discussed death and funerals out loud, in a group of people. And especially the idea of planning funerals. (They are adventurous enough to come to your house, open enough to explore a new idea.) Coffee and cake are great relaxers.

After the neighborly chit-chat period, it's probably your responsibility to open up the discussion. You're as nervous as everyone else. A thoughtful way to begin is to acknowledge, "Talking about funerals is very hard. We've all been to some. Maybe we've had to arrange some. I hope we can go beyond just talking, though, and help each other to think about our own funerals, just what we would like to have done with our bodies.

"Because it's hard to think about it," you might continue, "I thought I might help us get started by talking about the first time I was ever aware of death. Maybe others can think about that, and we can all say something." Then you tell about the time grandma got ill, you were only three; you can still smell the flowers; your mother puts you on her lap and talks; grandma is gone and you don't see her again; that's the very first memory! We all have such first memories in common; it's a good human beginning, the recollection of early experiences. Some people may have two or three experiences to relate. Go around in the circle, but let some say, "No, I'll pass." Once again, the important thing is to get started talking.

The group you gather about you may be more prepared than this group we've just talked about. Sharing such simple life-experiences, however, shows a roomful of friendly people how important death has been in their lives. Various ethnic customs may reveal themselves.

After everyone who wants to has shared, you might just as well talk about why you decided to plan your own funeral. Talk about the time you suddenly had to arrange Aunt Bessie's funeral and how much it cost, how upset everyone was and how you wished things could have been simpler. Tell your whole true story without embellishment. Tell about your resolve "back then" to do things differently as far as you and your own body are concerned. You will find others agreeing with your recitation of experience. Others may wish to offer adult stories from their own lives or the lives of acquaintances. You are on your way.

Don't let the meeting go on too late. Keep it short; end when it's high. "Do you think we should meet again soon?" Tell your friends you're sending for some memorial society literature for ideas and that maybe the next meeting could look at it. Ask for a good time of the week for the next meeting, agree on a place. (People who wait until later to set the meeting rarely do.) Ask if people would like to invite their friends, or would they prefer to do some more thinking together before they do that? These last questions are what sales people call "closers." They push people over the edge into commitment. They are important.

If you can't conduct a meeting in this general spirit, it's probably a good idea for you to get a friend who *can* lead the meeting. Very simple leadership is necessary, but simple or not, it cannot be sidestepped. On this subject, if it seems too hard for you to take this leadership role, be honest with yourself. (Getting it started is "plenty enough.")

There Is Useful Literature

The main source of encouragement to groups wishing to form memorial societies is the Continental Association of Funeral and Memorial Societies.

The Association is a federation. It does not start "branches." It welcomes the independent, autonomous local groups into membership in a common association with other similar groups. Through the Association, new groups secure help and sustenance; older groups share experience.

The Program of a Typical Memorial Society

The memorial society is the simplest form of cooperative. Neighbors and friends, joined together, and reaching out to new members, help each other with the simplest and yet most complex of life's tasks: funeral planning.

With the help of the Continental Association, your memorial society exists and you have announced its existence to the community. While the approaches are different from town to town, many societies will offer the following minimum program to its members:

1. By filling out a simple application form, a membership is added to the group. The fee may be as low as $5 or as much as $20. Some memorial societies charge $5 for a single member, $10 for a couple and $15 or $20 for a family with children. It is a one-time membership fee: once you are a member, you are always a member. Some societies have record-keeping charges, but these are low. When the society has become a member of the Continental group, your individual membership is transferable to another society in another part of the country, should you decide to move.

2. When you become a member, the services of the society are opened to you. Many societies will send you a copy of Morgan's *Manual of Death Education and Simple Burial,* copies of planning forms to guide you in your planning, a folder or two about the local society, perhaps a pamphlet from the nearest Eye Bank. No one can force you actually to work on and complete the planning forms, of course, but, when they are completed, you may send a copy to the memorial society for safekeeping.

3. By joining the memorial society, you are identifying yourself with good sense in the management of personal affairs as well as with a movement of people throughout the United States and Canada who believe in low-cost and dignified funerals and who advocate advance planning toward that end. It is good to work with others, and it is exciting to realize that you are part of a half-million-member movement. You are no longer alone in your advocacy of good sense.

4. You play a part in the conduct of your memorial society's operation through its annual meeting. At that time, you will hear reports

of officers, a financial statement, committee reports and the like. You have a "say" in operations, including a chance to elect members to the board of directors. Some day you might wish to run for office yourself! The annual meeting may also have a speaker, a debate or some interesting opportunity to expand your thinking.

5. Because of the usual voluntary and low-budget nature of the organization, many memorial societies have no formal offices as such and use the address of one of the officers for the organization's mailing purposes. That officer may well have his telephone listed as the society's, too. It is important for members to have a number to call: sometimes, if a death occurs, and no papers can be found, survivors will call for information. Many absolute strangers will call to talk about death and possible membership in the society. Local newspaper and radio people will thus have a number to call, too, if they have somehow been inspired to do a feature about the society.

6. The local group will usually have some cooperative arrangements with a local funeral director or two who will agree to work with its members, offering lower prices for the simpler funerals usually desired by memorial society members. If the group is unable to develop such a price list for its members, it still has an important advisory role for members, aiding them in planning.

7. The local society will participate in the affairs of the Continental group, helping to elect a board of directors. Members may attend the national gatherings of Continental, too, to which delegates from societies all over the country come to assess the progress of funeral reform and to consider the programs and direction of the overall movement.

Societies can fly as high as their ambitions and energy will permit. Writing in the January 1974 issue of *California Co-op Leadership,*[7] Florence E. Parker, executive secretary of the San Diego society[8] and a pioneer in the field, said that the society "includes persons of all denominations and many who have no church affiliation." She reported a San Diego membership total, as of November 1, 1973, of 8,331 memberships, covering some 14,376 persons, "almost evenly divided between single persons and couples." She said that minor dependent children and grandchildren living at home are covered by the parents' membership until they are twenty-one.

Parker's report clearly shows the advantage of group buying: "The society has an exclusive contract with one mortician who has been serving members for 13½ years and who gives them what is believed to be unique among memorial societies—a price guaranteed against inflation. The member sets forth his wishes for disposal of his body in a 5" × 7" booklet which also contains a contract with the mortician showing services he will render and price charged. Once this is signed by the mortician, the price is frozen; it has remained at $150 since January 1, 1964, despite rise in prices generally." Parker makes it clear that there is no conventional funeral service under the plan and that "the society encourages members to have a memorial service honoring memory of the dead, for its psychological and therapeutic value." Members are also given information about bequeathals of bodies to science and donation of organs for transplant.

That is one society; it chose its path. Yours can choose *its* paths. Size and strength always allow for more interesting opportunities for service. Consider the San Diego group reported above: it has enough members to allow for the unusual. A file of members who have cemetery property they no longer need is kept and word is distributed among members periodically. "If there is an inquiry," Parker reported, "buyer and seller are brought together; they make their own terms." She added, "This is a real service, for once you have bought cemetery property you are stuck with it."

Another valued and sensitive program is described in the report, which can be followed by any society, whether large or small. "When a member dies, after a decent interval to allow for recovery from shock, survivors receive a handwritten note expressing sympathy and inquiring if the mortician's service was satisfactory. A self-addressed stamped envelope is enclosed. This serves a four-fold purpose: it shows bereaved families that someone is watching and someone cares, and it gives them a chance to air any grievances, real or fancied. It also gives the society an opportunity to answer or explain, if necessary. It likewise serves to keep the mortician on his mettle, for he is aware of the society's practice."

The San Diego society, obviously an aggressive and forward-looking one, reaches out. It recently co-sponsored with a religious group a workshop entitled, "Ministering to Grief," in which clergymen of all faiths in San Diego County were invited to participate. The well-attended meeting helped clergymen to clarify their thoughts, to share experience and, of course, to learn more about the society. There are, indeed, as many things to do as imagination and time will permit.

Fred Nora, the effective editor of *California Co-op Leadership,* told (in the same issue that included the San Diego report) of a program of Berkeley, California's Bay Area Funeral Society,[9] which highlights the unusual extent to which cooperative people can go to help each other. The Bay Area group includes, among many services to members, the scattering of ashes at a cost of $25, from a small plane. Paul Wittig, the pilot, who donates his time to this service, took Nora on a flight to scatter a member's ashes in the Pacific Ocean, remarking that he wished more members were aware of the program.

And so it goes. More than one hundred groups are affiliated with Continental, each with its own program. They find mutual strength and support in their common affiliation with Continental.

It May Begin with a Memorial Society—But Does It Need to End There?

A person loved wants more love. A consumer with a little control over his affairs wants more control. It seems quite reasonable that he should.

Among some members of memorial societies there is a restiveness which looks beyond present usefulness, beyond present valuable services to another point in future time, when consumers will exercise even more control.

One might ask if there is more that consumers can do than organize memorial societies. Aren't these enough? What more can be done?

Looking Ahead:
The Ideal Conversation
with the Ideal Consumer

4

"Community Funeral Home. This is Tim Jones."

"Hello, Tim. This is Mary Thompson. John just died. Doctor Brown is here now, and he's just leaving. I thought I'd call you right away."

"Mary, I'm so sorry. You and John have been such good members of our group. We will miss him. He was a real friend."

"Thank you, Tim. He *was* a popular man, there's no question about it. You know, we have to find a good time for the memorial meeting."

"Look, let me get your file and our calendar. It'll take just a moment."

"Sure, go ahead, Tim." . . .

"I'm back. That didn't take long. I've got John's file. Of course, you know his wishes. We'll pick up his body in about half an hour and take it to the Johnson Medical Center. Bill—he just came in a minute ago—is taking care of the necessary permits and papers. Don't worry about them. Uh, let's see. How about this Sunday? Saturday, you know, we're having that big meeting for "friends of friends," to talk about our cooperative. But on Sunday, there's lots of room, all afternoon in fact. Would you want to reserve that time?"

"I think Sunday would be fine. Mr. Bailey, the new minister over at our church, I don't know if you've met him yet, has been so helpful while John has been ill. He's here now, and he wants to plan a little gathering at the church after the morning service for me, so our friends can get together. I'll tell them all to come over to the Home that afternoon, where his friends from work, some of his fraternity brothers, our neighbors will come. Maybe some of the church people will like the idea of a memorial meeting instead of a funeral; but they're not too—well, used to the idea. Maybe we'll even get a few members. John talked and talked for years to the people there, but seeing's believing, isn't it?"

"Sure, I've met the minister. He came in to see us when he arrived in town. We arranged for a transfer of his membership from the funeral society he used to belong to, to ours. He's a very fine man. . . . How many seats do you think we'll need for our meeting, Mary?"

"Oh, about seventy-five or so. There are a lot of people."

"Well, you know we could always open the sliding door in the big room if the group gets too large and bring in some chairs from the downstairs quiet room."

"That's true. Is the slide projector there?"

"Yes, we had it over at the junior high school the other day for a discussion group, but it's back now. Want to use it?"

"I think so. John and I were just looking over the slides a couple of nights ago. It might be nice to show them to our friends."

"Mary, I remember when you and John came to visit and we talked about arrangements for death. You were both so emphatic that you wanted a memorial meeting. You told me you had both stayed up all night talking about donating your bodies to the Medical Center. You thought I would try to argue about it, remember, and were you surprised when I pulled some of the Center forms out of my desk and helped you fill them out, witnessed them myself!"

"Well, you know, we were pretty new members, then. Sometimes you don't really believe things until you actually are there. You have a good memory, Tim."

"Mary, let me get a few things moving here and I'll drop by at the house later today. Will you be in around four?"

"Sure, I'll be here. Do come by. I'll work up a list of people in the meantime we really need to call. I called Edwina just before I called you and she said the Home's Social Service will be glad to call up our friends. I'm really so, so tired. She said she'll arrange some refreshments for the memorial meeting and, if I decide to visit Ma next week in Dallas, she'll see to it that someone comes by to feed the dog."

"Mary, we've got to do these things together. Look, I'll see you later and we can talk some more about Sunday's plans. If you need me before I get over, just give me a call. Do you need anything from the store?"

"No, thanks, Tim. Someone on Edwina's committee is picking up some cream for me, so I'll be able to give some coffee and cake to people who stop by today and tomorrow. She's a fine lady, Tim, we're lucky to have her."

"We're fortunate, Mary, every one of us. See you later. Bye."

A Consumer Alternative

Those few minutes on the telephone represent a complete revolution in values. They represent a changed attitude toward the funeral home; it is one of friendship and genuine service. The people are friends; Mary is comfortable. Tim, the funeral director, is helpful. Mary expects help from him; he expects to offer it. It is a civilized exchange. There is no talk of money. Mary knows the costs are within her reach because she and John talked about arrangements and costs years before. She is not apprehensive. (Indeed, she may have prepaid the funeral costs in the special escrow accounts maintained by the Home for those members wanting to get everything ready, including money, ahead of time.)

The neighborly exchange in this new setting is powerful. Mary called Edwina, knowing the Social Service group would want to be helpful: she may have known Edwina personally, but it would not have been necessary. It is possible that Edwina's phone number, representing Social Service, was near Mary's phone, along with the Home's number. The Home provides the focus for a gathering of the community. Mary thinks about tomorrow, not only the tragedy that has overtaken her. There is no effort to sell her anything. She and John both knew what they wanted, the Home knew it, and that is exactly what will be offered. Note the offers of help from Tim. He means it. It is his job. That is what the Home is all about: the transformation of old institutions, the replacement of old stifling attitudes with new and forward-looking ones.

The essential strength of the phone conversation is that Mary was following through on earlier planning, and so was the Home. Mary could have made other plans; it just happened that Mary and John wanted to donate their bodies to medical science. Cremation, earth burial, a wake, whatever they wanted would have been available. The Home lived out its expectation in helping Mary and John with their initial planning, with the saving of funds, perhaps, with the conduct of the occasion itself, with the meeting of immediate needs, and by permitting freedom of choice.

What if the Consumer Has Not Planned?

But what about Joe, who had not planned? Genevieve has died. She had not planned, either. What is the proper response of the Home under those circumstances?

"Community Funeral Home. This is Tim Jones."

"Mr. Jones, this is Joe Sampson. I don't think we've met. My wife, Genevieve, has just died. I'm not a member of the Home, so I was wondering if you could tell me where I can get help. We've lived here in town for only a few years. A fellow over at work, Abe Blue, had mentioned you sometime ago, but Genevieve and I didn't want to get into it that much. And now she's dead."

"Sure, Abe Blue's a member. Listen, Mr. Sampson, I want to make something very clear. Our Home was built to serve its members, but a few years ago we discussed the reluctance of a lot of people to talk about death, and we decided that we would give the staff permission to accept a family membership even at the moment when death arrangements are being made. Later on, the membership committee could pass on the application. Would you want to become a member? You do seem to know a little about us, and that's good."

"Well, I tell you, Mr. Jones . . ."

"Tim is all right, if I can call you Joe."

"Tim, fine. I do need your help. Genevieve and I don't like funeral parlors and funeral directors, excuse me, you know, the private-profit fellas, and maybe that's why we haven't talked about the whole business much. She and I both want simple funerals but, uh, well, we both want to be cremated. You're not for that, I'm sure."

"Look, Joe, maybe half of our members want cremation."

"Really, well, I guess I don't know much about you. Maybe we can get together. What do I do now? Genevieve's body is at the hospital."

"Joe, I will have a member of our staff go over to the hospital and make the necessary arrangements. When can we get together? Would you be free in an hour? I can come over and we can talk about what you'd like. Where do you live?"

"Tim, I live . . ."

And so it went. Tim visited Joe at the Sampson house, learned that the couple didn't like the idea of body viewing, and they didn't like the idea of memorial meetings, either. Joe was going to have friends and co-workers over to his house in a couple of nights for a kind of gathering; he could use a couple dozen folding chairs. Genevieve's body would be taken directly to the crematory, and her ashes were to be distributed in their garden, which Genevieve had loved so much.

This ideal conversation with a consumer not as yet connected with the Home reflects the quality of the approach. Joe knew enough not even to discuss prices: Abe Blue had probably told him that what he needed he would pay for and there would be no pushing for higher sales volume. While Joe's needs were relatively slight, and he would not be too demanding of time and services, he was nevertheless made welcome. Tim's job was to help. Joe did become a member and was grateful for the understanding and support he needed. The Social Service group, following Tim's discussion with Joe, would bring in some food for the gathering of friends at Joe's house, so Joe could concentrate on greeting his saddened visitors.

The Full Service of Consumers

The proper role of a consumer-owned facility is full service to consumers. Its focus is naturally to serve members, but people can become members (if the Home arranges things that way) at any point along the way. Even though Joe and Genevieve had not made their plans known ahead of time, their wishes gradually emerged in discussions with Joe, permitting the staff to respond sensitively.

It is the idea of full service that historically pushes consumers into consideration of "next steps." Full service means full control of the process, no matter the field, in which the consumer is engaged.

Consumers engaged in a nonprofit distribution of foodstuffs, if their volume is sufficient, wonder if they should do their own trucking. Then the warehouse idea comes into the picture, with a view to controlling the middleman relationship. Then come questions about the ownership of the food-processing plants, the canneries. Then, logically, consumers should negotiate with the farmers directly and —an even more avant-garde notion—consumers should own the farms. Lots of arguments erupt along the edges of our minds, but an idea has its own life, its own exegesis.

With such control comes a sense of controlling prices and quality. Negotiation with owners is one step. To become the owners is the last step on the ladder.

So it is in the funeral picture. Consumers first feel their frustrations in personal dealings with the Funeral Establishment. Then they share those feelings with others. Concern about high prices, about buying unwanted goods and services, about the sense of pressure leads to the development of memorial societies. Through the act of planning, a consumer who knows what he wants thus becomes freer to exercise, or have exercised on his behalf, his own wishes. A funeral director thus has some restriction or restraints placed on him by the consumer who has planned.

Consumers who have planned their own funerals expect their wishes to be respected, not only by their survivors but by funeral parlors themselves. The search for friendly funeral directors follows. Arrangements are made with one or more who agree to respect the planning agreements and who may, in fact, spell out the costs and details of low-cost funerals and agree to offer these to memorial society members.

A memorial society is a positive program. It is forward-looking. It is an important step in the direction of consumer sovereignty.

A Memorial Society Is Good, but Not Enough

There are limitations in the memorial-society idea which must be weighed. Many have already been sensed by organizers and members. Others have been perceived by a few. These should be generally understood, not only by members of memorial societies but also by those just entering the ranks of funeral reform.

What are those limitations?

The memorial society, resting as it does on the advocacy of advance planning and the negotiation of low-cost funerals with funeral directors, is *dependent* on the private-profit Funeral Establishment. If every citizen of the United States planned a low-cost funeral, there is a good possibility it would not be delivered by funeral directors, since *they are in charge of the funeral marketplace.*

The ability of the memorial society to offer low-cost funerals through contract or agreement is directly related to its ability to find a maverick in the herds of directors. Such individuals are difficult to round up, and only a relative few will be prepared to cooperate.

Legal compulsion is difficult. It is unlikely that the industry will ever be required to cooperate by those legal authorities and supervising agencies responsible for supervising the funeral industry, since they are dominated by the practitioners of the trade. Their codes of ethics are self-determined. Legislation compelling cooperation is unlikely, since funeral lobbyists are powerful and legislators generally too responsive to the needs of businessmen.

A hundred or five hundred or a thousand memorial societies, performing useful services, still do not modify the general funeral situation. A memorial society helps only its members. The cooperating funeral director is free to follow his traditional pursuits in traditional ways with every other customer. The memorial society is in no position to exercise restraints on the way the funeral director does business with others.

The pursuit and provision of salvation for the individual, through low-cost funerals and the sense of satisfaction that planning provides, side-steps the need for reformation of the industry itself. Many individuals, concerned about the funeral industry as a whole, have their energy and passion defused by their membership and activity in a memorial society: they relax; they have found an answer for themselves. They will dispose of their own bodies decently and at low expense. But what about the millions of people elsewhere, who have no memorial societies, who don't know about the benefits of advance planning? The answer, as it has been stated up to now, is that those millions should start memorial societies.

However, memorial-society organization per se, no matter how extensive, (and this is important for concerned people to understand) does not necessarily contribute to the change needed in the overall marketplace. It contributes only to the salvation of those particular individuals who have created or found memorial societies and leaves the others out in the cold.

For all the blather from funeral directors about the problems to their industry posed by memorial societies, no threat is actually posed, since few societies go beyond the planning/low-cost-deal function. In fact, where a memorial society makes an exclusive relationship with one or two funeral directors, the directors benefit through higher volume. They may receive less money per funeral, but they receive more business. The American funeral situation, beset by too many funeral directors and not enough business for each one, makes a successful businessman out of the director who can work out such a deal with a society.

Memorial society activity creates an illusion about funeral reform without the substance one might wish. One can state correctly, on the other hand, that food co-ops, by making consumers their own businessmen, that co-op farm supply houses, providing member-farmers their own needs, that insurance co-ops and the dozens of other cooperative forms, helping members with their needs, actually do modify the marketplace, since new structures are created in which business is done. Were a group of neighbors to form a food co-op and proceed to the local A & P to negotiate a slight reduction, we might laugh and think it not worth their while. But they could do a real job by going directly to a wholesaler for their supplies and get a much larger reduction. By replacing the A & P with their own organization, they would reduce their dependency on the A & P as well as their expenses. Memorial societies are like that group going to the A & P manager: they petition the funeral director for a reduction and continue their dependency on him.

When a memorial society works out an agreement with a funeral director for lower costs for its members, it generally accepts the low price that is offered. What else can it do? The funeral director, notwithstanding the advantage of greater volume, may complain that he is not making money on the deal. But curiously enough, he goes along.

The memorial society, because of its tangential and dependent relationship to the funeral industry, has no idea of the actual cost/price situation in the funeral business and is in no position to know what is fair—whether the $500 could be $300 or $250. The funeral director is not likely to bare the secrets of his trade to the memorial society, since he is active and busy with hundreds of other unenlightened bodies from nonmemorial-society sources.

Government Ownership?

Control through a regulatory agency at the governmental level is a weak sister, since such agencies traditionally have been manned by personnel from, or sympathetic to, the industry being regulated. The likelihood of consumer dominance on such commissions, while desirable, is improbable at the present time.

Perhaps the answer is outright government ownership.

Such ownership is always an option. Should the government accept responsibility for the disposal of bodies in dignity—as it has supervised our marriages and recorded our children's births—there is a quick end to our complaining. Citizens could have their influence on government policy in this field through the legislative and administrative process, as well as by service on advisory committees and commissions. There would not necessarily be unemployment among funeral directors, since they would be hired by government to do at a salary that which they are doing now in a private-profit framework.

Automobile inspection comes to mind. In New York State such required inspection is done through private garages. Abuse is widespread, because of the propensities of private-profit operators, who may either exaggerate an auto's need for repairs or pass through blindly a friend's automobile. In New Jersey, on the other hand, the process of inspection is conducted in state-owned and -operated inspection facilities. Private profit cannot be a factor. No recommendations are made about dealers who will fix cars to meet inspection standards. It is free of the taint. If funeral operations were state or federal matters, they would be free of the taint.

Proposals for government ownership and operation need to be

considered in their context. Many people would protest such a move because it denies the right of a person to enter a field and to make money in it. Others would remind us of the overblown and inefficient bureaucracies that characterize much government operation today. Some would say that the government-owned funeral business would not be able to pay for itself and thus consumers would be contributing to yet another welfare-state operation, in which the extra funds needed to operate the facilities (beyond consumer payment for their use) would need to come from our taxes. And still others would say that our government is traditionally designed to support private-business operations and is not likely to take over a major industry in that way, particularly if it is succeeding. (When private business fails, as in the case of the railroads, government handouts seem to be assumed and acceptable.)

The central difficulty in proposals for government operations relates to the consumer himself. He is in no way engaged in the determination of policy affecting him. Certainly, he can offer his counsel in an advisory way. He can elect in and elect out governments. But he is confronted with a no-choice situation. What citizen feels he controls the State Department, the Social Security Administration, and so on? He is once again a recipient, destined to survive at the mercy of another large force. Once dependent on the whims and sales capacity of the Funeral Establishment, he would move into a situation where he would have only those choices prescribed him by government.

Were our governments in fact to be consumer-oriented, were government commissions to be manned by consumer representatives, were the influences of private industry spokesmen and representatives to be barred from government deliberations, the discussion could take on an entirely different form.

However, the actual mutual feeding relationship of government and private business, in which each nourishes and supports the other for the sake of each, has little room for consumer input, outside of the vote-gathering and illusions of tokenism we can observe today. That all of this mutual activity is at the direct expense of the consumer, in his role either as purchaser or as citizen, heightens the sense of frustration of those who would seek a more definitive role for the consumer.

The Choice Is Clear

No one wants to venture in new directions without thoroughly exhausting all the possibilities.

For the consumer, eager for solution, there seems to be little choice.

If full service, honest pricing, nonexploitation and the democratic engagement of the consumer in matters that affect him are guiding principles, the strongest, most logical argument would appear to be for activity which fulfills those ends: the operation of consumer-owned and consumer-controlled funeral houses.

Let us review carefully, and in summary, the alternatives.

One might pray for the private-profit Funeral Establishment to change its ways, ridding itself of the abuses of confidence that occur every day. However, just as petitions are not likely to induce the automobile folks to produce a safe car, there is little likelihood that funeral directors would respond to an appeal to conscience. The funeral director would have to open wide his books, tell us his costs and how he develops his price structure, post funeral choices for all to see and end his heavy sales pitch.

On the other hand, as we have discussed, consumer control over funeral directors might be exercised through some form of public control. Existing commissions, like most regulatory commissions, are servants of the industry, for they are manned largely by funeral directors themselves. To bow to consumer demands that such commissions be dominated by a majority of consumer representatives is to ask government and the trade to admit the impossible, that they have indeed been unconcerned with consumer needs and wishes. It will take many years for that transition to take place.

Protective and disclosure legislation, while desirable, is not a possibility on which we could depend. Were legislators to restrict earnings or in any way limit the "right to price" and a variable "fee for service" characteristic of groups calling themselves professional, they would find doctors, lawyers, accountants, psychologists and a dozen other groups pounding at their doors. Legislators, often themselves lawyers, are not fools. They are political animals.

Logically, some will argue at this point, the government should take over the funeral industry. That's the only way to take care of this mess. But, under some American conditions, as we have seen, can one hope that this would provide consumer engagement, the lowering of prices or the uplifting of moral and sales standards? Governments tend to represent citizens, not involve them in their own welfare. Thus, the consumer would remain dependent, perhaps more dependent than before, with no alternative whatsoever. Because of its long-time preoccupation with encouraging private profit, the government is not likely to take over a successful industry. Were the funeral parlors failing, and the practitioners flying to other work, that would be another matter. No, the answer is not here.

Surely consumer education is the answer. (Too often, when consumerists lack ideas about where to turn or about how a problem might be solved, they put the burden on the consumer. This maintains the *caveat emptor* posture we discussed earlier. Again we need to refocus on *caveat venditor,* putting the responsibility on the shoulders of the seller.) Consumer educationists would argue: inform the consumer. Show him the score card. But, as everyone will readily admit, the impact of sorrow and pressure at the time of death is indeed great: one's education and training and consumer instincts tend to fall by the wayside. The answer for society is not here.

Then, there is the alternative we have already outlined: let us negotiate with the funeral director. Let us join together in consumer associations and protect our members from the abuses of the marketplace. This is, in fact, what memorial societies have done. Through the practice of advance planning, thus forestalling the impact of pressure salesmanship, and through forms of collective bargaining with funeral directors, assuring lower prices for members, these consumers have found answers for themselves. The creation, support and use of memorial societies are the first victory in the first battle with the funeral marketplace. Their impact is monumental, for they demonstrate the power of unity. Their educational significance is beyond measurement.

But, alas, it is only a beginning. Memorial societies do not transform the funeral marketplace. The business remains the same: it is still free to exploit those who are not members of memorial societies. Its freedom-to-sell has been modified slightly and then only for memorial-society people. These groups, which have done so much to help individuals, have not moved into the area of effective social justice, through the actual transformation of offending institutions into nonoffending ones.

Practical responses, universal in scope, fundamental in nature are required. Considering these alternatives, there is really no way for the consumer to move but in the direction of ownership and operation of funeral facilities.

The ideal conversation with the ideal consumer which we overheard earlier becomes more and more alive and possible. It seems to suggest the way things really ought to be. What might have seemed visionary at first, even wildly utopian, as we opened our discussion, becomes perhaps the only option. It moves closer and closer to the top of the human and social agenda.

Getting friends and neighbors together for such a purpose is a big job. But it is rewarding. For at the end of the road is true consumer satisfaction.

The first little steps toward giant solutions are the most difficult. But we can be sure they will be more exciting and ultimately more significant than taking giant steps toward what turn out to be little solutions.

First Steps Toward
Consumer Ownership:
The Board and the Membership

5

The decision has been made. You will try to organize a consumer-owned and consumer-controlled funeral establishment. You have thought about it long enough to feel that you will yourself stick with the project for as long as is needed to complete the work, and even more important, you are willing to talk about it with friends and strangers. Too, you are prepared to have people talk about you, the idea you have and the progress of the idea without your being there. That does happen to people who step out of the ordinary and try to do something different; the words said about you may not always be nice words, either.

Everyone Will Not Work with You

It is important for people who venture into social pioneering to be willing to accept (if not understand) indifference and sometimes active opposition. Sometimes you learn that your friends will turn against you, saying all kinds of things: "All he talks about now is death and funeral parlors." Or, "It's a rotten idea. I don't even want to see him anymore."

An organizer of something new and different might expect difficulty, in our case from the Funeral Establishment, but it is harder for the excited worker in a good cause to deal with the sometimes strange and even hostile attitudes of the people you called friends. Private planning is tolerated: it's quiet and not visible. But when you go "bricks and mortar," "go public," you are displaying your loyalties on your sleeve. That is hard for many people—and it will take some courage.

Everyone will not jump on the bandwagon. Many people, perhaps most, are reluctant to join something new. They would rather wait and see. You were like that once, too. It is probably a better use of your time to let the experience, momentum and, hopefully, success of your project convince these people. You could waste days and days of your time trying to convince someone and, presuming you succeed, still wind up with only one more supporter.

Apathy is a miserable nit. Otherwise fine and thoughtful people may not seem to give a damn about what you're doing. Sometimes they just don't seem to be interested in anything. Avoid social-work notions: don't try to engage them in your project for their good, for the sake of their souls. Should you be able to get them to your first meetings, you may find them to be exceedingly weak reeds on which to depend. This virulent social disease is not overcome by a couple of aspirins. It edges away for a meeting or two and then returns in force, usually just at the time you might get to depend on that person, expecting him to write a letter, to visit the editor of your newspaper, to make a telephone call. The person you are "saving" cannot be depended on. Hold that person for a later time. Keep him on a potential-member list, as a potential beneficiary of your program. But don't even depend on interest then.

Apathy is such a serious problem that it deserves special treatment. Those of us who are concerned with community development, with making our cities, towns and neighborhoods better places in which to live have to recognize the large measure we have in ourselves. We need to respond with sympathy: we were there once. (Some of us chronic organizers might well have had nightmares of calling a big conference to discuss the subject, but no one came!)

A group of students discussing the problem in a college course in consumer education offered several explanations for the phenomenon. The instructor, seeking to make the discussion as rewarding as possible, suggested that students not speak to the question, "Why are people apathetic?" but rather, "Why am I that way?" Among the frank explanations were, offered at first reluctantly but then with keen interest, the following: fear of being called a "kook" by friends; question whether or not a few people could get anything done, anyway; the political and economic control by a few is too strong for effective action by small groups; uncertainty about what needed to be done; questions about personal capacity; nervousness about working with others; fear of one's own weaknesses and incapacities becoming apparent to other people; reluctance to speak in groups; worry that all the responsibility will fall on the person himself, if he "gets involved"; frank admissions of laziness; enjoying life too much to become involved in "causes"; not wanting to be called a fanatic and, presumably, not wanting to think of oneself as a fanatic; too young to be respected by older people. All of these reasons, and many more, are difficult to acknowledge in ourselves, where they apply.

There is another kind of friend who will wait until someone else starts something. He will be second. He will always be second. (*You* are fated to be first.) It is no wonder people form groups, because groups help most "seconders" to nudge each other onward. Sometimes, though, the seconder won't work for your cause until there are a dozen, or twenty or five hundred people. When his estimates of the number of people needed even to get started get too high, it is probably good advice to let that person wait for a while before being drawn into the enterprise. Such people undervalue the importance of the first person and are likely to be "the last people to be good," waiting for everyone else to become so first. These people need the courage of the convictions of too many people to be effective.

When it comes to working on a consumer-owned and consumer-controlled funeral home, you will find friends who suddenly remember old Uncle Matthias, a decent guy, who was a funeral director. They will be reluctant to embarrass Aunt Jane, his widow, by becoming active in something that might seem critical of the work funeral directors are doing now. It is also possible that some of your friends may have personal friends among funeral directors, and they do not want to face that ultimate confrontation when their director-friend asks them "why they did it."

Some friends will oppose you for philosophical reasons. (See Chapter 2, "Change Is Not Easy.")

For all of these friends, there is little you can do except to say to them, in a friendly and firm way, "I'm sorry you won't join us. It's an important idea. Maybe later you'll want to join us, when you're ready." Sometimes these friends will become dropouts in your life, if they are strongly opposed; your real friends will stay with you, regardless.

Where, then, do you look? Which friends will help? For whom are you looking?

The organizers of new ventures do themselves a favor when they focus on identifying in their communities those people who are already concerned with funeral reform, who are personally troubled by experiences they may have had, who are people with experience in beginning (relatively fearlessly) new groups, who are already in some measure community leaders. There *are* outspoken people, strong people, members of boards of directors of established groups, writers of letters to the editor, able but currently inactive people who have been muttering about getting back into the swing of things.

Identification is the job.

That's why an existing memorial society is such a splendid base for the development of a consumer funeral facility, for the members of the memorial society have broken the first barriers: they have planned their own funerals, they have joined with others in an organization that believes in planning, they have identified themselves with a measure of funeral reform.

Many of these people will be too busy to work with you. That's all right. They will be friends in the wings, often available to step on stage if there's a crisis, if you need specialized help or advice, ready to share their experience with you over a cup of coffee.

There are other busy types who are ready for a change. The old causes for which they have worked may not need them anymore. They were getting to the point where the excitement of doing something new is fading away, anyway. It is time (and they will say this if they are good community developers) for the work to be passed on to others, who know now how to do it and who need a chance to carry the responsibility themselves.

Then there are those who believe in what you are doing or want to do but who have never surfaced as community leaders. You may be providing just the right kind of opportunity for those persons, who may have many skills: business organization, administration, book-keeping and accounting, public-speaking ability, writing experience, teaching skills. Their regular work may have kept them busy and the right after-hours cause not come along. You should not hesitate to ask such people. They will often feel honored for having been asked.

Identifying concerned and capable people in your community, people who feel that "something should be done," is a major responsibility. It is the first big task you have. But they are there, as sure and as evident as are the apathetic ones, the ones to be second, the people opposed to the idea.

It is extremely important, when approaching potential leaders, to emphasize the importance of strong leadership, in the beginning, when things are getting started. If they are the leaders you think they may be, they will understand. It is a good idea to talk about the *first* board of directors, the *organizing* board of directors, the *interim* group to get things started. Capable people, with many challenges available to them everywhere, may see the importance of another group like yours in the community, but they will not want to be chained to it forever. Emphasize the significance of a special kind of leadership in the beginning. From the members who will be brought into the established organization will come new board members, so that the creative pioneers you are seeking and do need, indeed, can be assured of their eventual freedom for other tasks calling them.

Now That You Have Your First Organizers . . .

Call them the organizing committee. Call them the interim board of directors. Call them the steering committee. It doesn't matter much; the function is usually the same: to get the show on the road.

There is no magic number for this group's size. It should be large enough to allow for a division of labor; it should be small enough to let friendships develop and confidence of people in each other to grow.

Try seven people. Maybe the group will feel confident that they have the time and ability to solve the organizing problems. On the other hand, they may feel the need for more input from other people. Try eleven, then. If the 7–11 gambit doesn't work, aim for fifteen. Hesitate before getting larger than that. The biggest living room or the smallest conference room available to you can help you decide.

These people are now in your living room (if that's where you decide to meet) for their first meeting, to consider the question of organizing a consumer facility (and you hope they'll serve on the first organizing board). Or perhaps they have already agreed to do so because you screwed up your courage enough to ask them and to invite them to the first meeting, at your house.

But they are there. The formality of first greetings and the necessity of coffee and cookies or cheese and crackers are over. People are talking to each other.

It is time to begin.

From Where Will the Members Come?

All right, you and your group have decided to establish a consumer facility. You have talked long enough and frequently enough about the dream that there is beginning to be, if there wasn't in the first place, a tone of some considerable conviction in your voices.

Someone will surely ask nervously, for the fifteenth time: Will enough people really be interested? It's late, since you already decided to proceed on that assumption, but it is not too late to ask questions of a lot of people that will relieve that uncertainty and would draw them into the circle.

It may be the moment to conduct a survey.

If you are part of a memorial society, the approach is easy. Ask each member, after explaining the basic proposal, for a response to key questions:

1. Does the member think a consumer-owned funeral home is a good idea?

2. Does the member think his friends will welcome the idea?

3. Does the member believe in it strongly enough to invest in the new organization? Would the member wish to consider lending funds to the organization for first expenses?

4. Does the member have a list of friends and associates who might respond to an invitation to join and invest in the new consumer facility?

These questions presume that a memorial society has decided to take the leap, own and operate property, and become an enlarged operation: a memorial society transforming itself into a funeral home. The society's incorporation papers will have to be examined to be sure that such ownership is possible. It may be necessary for a new corporation to be created, with the memorial society the sole stockholder.

An existing memorial society can expect to grow tremendously, once it enters the complete-service field. Relying as it once did on volunteers exclusively, the typical experience, it will now be moving into responsibility for property, into hiring and supervision of employees, into legally required benefits for employees and their families, into hospitalization and similar programs for employees, into virtually all the problems of owning and operating a business encountered by a single individual venturing into it for private-profit motives.

The more typical situation, since there are relatively few memorial societies, is for the people interested in a consumer facility to have to start from the very beginning. Such a consumer facility, let us call it the Cooperative Funeral Home, will incorporate the ideas and programs of a typical memorial society and will provide the services of a funeral home as well.

The survey as an instrument of *generating* interest and eventually members is an old ploy: it really works.

Every member of your organizing board should write down the name and address of every friend he has in town. All the names and addresses should be filed together in one file. Using a 3" × 5" card for each name will help you avoid overlapping: it's annoying to *receive* more than one survey of this rather specialized type. It will seem to the receiver that people were not paying much attention and were sending it out randomly to everyone.

After the friends, it's time to think of opinion-makers known to the group, whose support might mean something to you. There are local politicians, religious leaders, heads of organizations, society leaders like "wealthy old Mrs. Kimball on the West Side," newspaper publishers and editors, many people who—for a variety of reasons— might find it of value to themselves to talk about, know about and maybe even support the notion that people can do things for themselves. In appealing to these people for their support—or at least seeking to inform them—you are drawing on the power of the new consumerism. Few people, at least publicly, want to be known as opposed to the rights and welfare of consumers.

Decisions on how to inform and attract people will depend on your analysis of your local situation. In some situations, to work with friends alone—and their friends—will be enough. In others, to work without the established leadership of the community will be extremely difficult.

The survey form which asks the questions you have in mind should have a covering letter signed by the organizing board. Why? Because the recipient will find the names of friends there. The recipient will see that some form of organization exists (he isn't being asked to be a pioneer) and be pleased to be asked to associate with them all in such a worthwhile task.

The letter should be a basic description of the proposed plan the group has in mind. It should invite the interest of the reader in the idea and then, in a friendly way, draw attention to the survey form. A stamped reply envelope might be enclosed.

A sample letter follows:

COMMITTEE FOR A COOPERATIVE FUNERAL HOME

Dear Friend:

Many people in our community feel it is time that we consider the organization of a funeral home that would be owned and operated by consumers themselves. When we first talked, it seemed strange, but as we got into the question more and more, we felt we had "an idea whose time has come" for our community.

We would value your interest and support. Basically, a Cooperative Funeral Home would provide the following:

1. Funeral Planning: It would assist its members in the proper planning of their own funerals, aiding them to make decisions appropriate to their philosophy, income and style of life.

In that regard, the Home also would have all necessary forms available to its members, enabling contributions to be made to the Eye Bank, bodies to be donated to nearby medical research facilities, and so on.

The Home's officers and staff would be available to aid members and their families in filling out the forms. Files will be maintained in the Home for each member.

2. Funeral Services: The Home's facility would be available for the conduct

of the usual funeral but also have rooms available for those members wishing to have memorial meetings instead.

The Home will have available the services of fully trained and licensed funeral directors, who will be employed by our organization.

It would help the committee immeasurably if we could have the benefit of your thinking at this time. The enclosed survey form and stamped reply envelope will help you to give us your thoughts.

Sincerely,

(Signed by the members of the Committee)

A suggested survey form, leaving spaces for answers, would ask the following questions:

Do you think the Cooperative Funeral Home is essentially a good idea?
What do you see as its main strengths?
What do you see as its main weaknesses?
How do you think the community will respond to the service?

Members will be asked to pay a small membership fee, but some additional investment capital will be needed to finance the initial development.

Do you think we will have any difficult raising money for this kind of service?

Is it the kind of program to which you would lend financial support?

Do you think some of your friends and associates would respond warmly to this proposal?

At a later time, would you be willing to have us send a letter, perhaps over your signature, to your friends?

What items of general advice would you like to offer our organizing committee at this time?

Signed:_____

The Constituency

With these letters to your own friends and associates, you are on your way to building a constituency. While everyone is potentially a member, you know from experience, or will know, that everyone will not respond. You might (ignore the funereal pun) get a cold shoulder. If you can find your natural constituency, the people who share the idea, if you have identified the already aware constituency, you are on your way. The others will come along later. You do not need the entire community to begin. Start with that portion of the community that you have.

There are ready-made groups that should be drawn into the program in its earliest stages. Some of their representatives might well be on your initial organizing group.

For example, certain church groups will respond well to this opportunity. They may be troubled by the tendency of their members to spend too much at funeral time and want to emphasize the dignity of death and life instead of garish displays. Sensitive clergymen may wish to participate and will know those in their groups who would be naturally responsive to such efforts.

There are trade unions and fraternal orders, already concerned with the costs of death (since they usually have death benefits of some kind), who might welcome a better use of the death-benefit dollar.

There are farmer and consumer cooperatives, experienced with the idea of people working together for common ends, that will welcome this new form of cooperation.

There are already established consumer-education and -action organizations, whose lists of activist members may be a rich source of concerned people, eager to welcome yet another expression of consumer action.

There are antipoverty groups, in and out of government settings, that have constituencies. Within them, there are forward-looking organizers and administrators who are concerned about the long-range welfare of the poor families in your community.

There are specialized cooperatives, like credit unions, with leaders and members who may look kindly on this consumer do-it-yourself scheme.

Many of these groups have newsletters which can carry your story. Most have literature racks and programs. All have articulate leaders. All want to identify with consumers trying to solve their own problems. Few have wrestled adequately with the question of self-help in the funeral field, and they know it. Your organizing committee may be providing the first opportunity these groups have ever had to advise their members effectively in this field.

Some organizing committees, in addition to reaching potential supporters by mail and building a constituency that way, may wish to have an open meeting for leaders in the community, inviting people from many settings to share in the discussion. Such a meeting, providing solid information from the organizing committee about the basic proposal for the community, can generate social excitement, new board members, new committee members, and potential users of the service.

If the committee is itself set within the context of a church, trade union or other group with a natural constituency, the problem is much simpler. You are providing a service to your members, you can reach them easily, there are forums within the activity-life of such groups where leaders and potential members can be identified. Such a group, serving the natural members of an existing organization, can decide at an early time if its service will be limited only to its members or to its members plus outside people. To support a funeral home will require a rather large membership, and a study of death-patterns would have to be conducted. Most cooperative funeral home planning groups arising out of established groups will probably wish to keep membership open to the larger community, to be sure there is enough volume of business to keep the Cooperative Funeral Home operative.

There is a lot to be said for organizing the program to serve people in the entire community who wish to be members. For one thing, death strikes everyone. Everyone is subjected to the problems posed by the private-profit Funeral Establishment. Further, a useful, well-known, well-organized and run Cooperative Funeral Home, which anyone can join, is good strategy for your organization. You *believe* in helping the entire community and you *practice* it as well, by providing essential services.

The board and membership will want to study carefully the ideas and promises of cooperation. Mutual effort is not an accidental result of two or more people getting together. It is a stated intention and philosophy of life. There is a body of experience in the cooperative framework which should be studied and analyzed. There are existing cooperative movements with strength to lend.

The glamour of actually doing something about your own welfare —with a glimmer of its potential for hundreds and thousands and millions of people—will fade away unless attention is paid early in the game to the essential thoughts and experience in the cooperative field.

Certainly cooperatives can be formed without an idea structure, but they tend to be dry and listless. It is not mere money that in the long run captures the imagination and devotion of people, it is the sense of belonging, feeling useful, doing something for others.

The Working Philosophy
of a Consumer-owned
Facility

6

A membership organization is not the same as an organization created by a few to serve a larger group. Both can perform valuable functions in a community. A voluntary community ambulance corps would be an example of the latter. Providing an opportunity for a relative handful to develop skills and provide urgently needed service in a community, the ambulance corps may solicit funds from the public, its constituency, for operating expenses. But such supporters have no "say" in its operations. If you disagree with some policy or program, you just don't contribute.

A membership organization, built on cooperative ideas, provides an opportunity for every member to influence organizational policy. When the purpose is more than social and a business is being conducted, every member is part-owner of the enterprise.

The cooperative idea is basically an effort to establish democracy in business. We are accustomed to the idea of democracy in our political life: one person, one vote; "let the person speak"; a citizen can seek vote-support from other citizens and hold a public office. We do not, unless we are active in producer or consumer cooperatives, have the experience of economic democracy.

Corporate business life gives votes to shares, not to people. If you own ten shares, you have ten votes. Another person with one thousand shares has that many votes. Thus, control is in the hands of the wealthiest. Money is power. In a democratic business, owned and operated by its users, every person, regardless of the extent of investment, has an equal vote in the affairs of the cooperative.

The essential difference, of course, is that the cooperative is organized to serve its members, to provide the highest quality product or service at the lowest possible cost. Its motives are not motives of gain. Surely, the organization has to make enough money to pay its bills, but it is not defined to give income to those whose only contribution to the enterprise is providing money. Even capital loaned to the cooperative is supposed to receive dividends at a reasonable and fair level: the cooperative ought not to exist to provide anyone with an opportunity to make a "killing." Speculation is out.

There are two views about the significance of a cooperative conducting a business in a largely private-profit economy. One, the more conservative, says that the cooperative extends the benefits of private ownership to the masses. Every person becomes a capitalist when he joins a cooperative, from which, according to the extent he uses the cooperative, he receives a share of the profits. This view has been advanced largely by persons fearful of the cry of "socialist" or "communist," who have sought to Americanize and to make respectable the cooperative idea, which indeed was at one time the victim of concerted attacks—as a kind of socialism—by business-oriented groups.

The conservative view is perfectly sound if the cooperative people involved in such a view do not lose, in the course of wrapping the private enterprise flag about themselves, the precious social and humane insights of the older person-oriented philosophy.

The other view is the historic, international view of cooperation, which, taking a global glance at the human condition, argues that a new force is necessary in life's marketplaces which encourages neither enterprise for private gain nor compulsory activity by state mandate. Those, like the author, holding this position have come to the conclusion that the choices for society are not limited to two: capitalism or communism. Cooperation represents a third force, another way, which argues, unlike either of the other two ways of life or systems of thought, that the ultimate users, the consumers, are the logical owners of the enterprises serving them. The capitalist argues that businesses should be owned by those who have the money to invest in them, thus deserving—for having taken the risk—the right to share in the profits. In this philosophy the duty of consumers is merely to provide the marketplace. The communist argues that the state, as a repository of concern for the welfare of its citizens, should own and operate the central businesses essential to the survival of citizens.

In the United States both capitalist and statist drifts of thought exist among large segments of the population. The condition is aggravated by the notion held by many in the United States that the main, if not the sole, function of government is to assure the success of the private-profit marketplace. The capitalist argument is dominant. The airplane industry and the railroads—the very large industries that do not seem efficient enough to make money for the owners—want government financing. The organized welfare poor ask the state to provide more and do more. Except for the very rich and the very poor, most people seem to opt for the idea that government should see to it that private enterprise works. Even consumer-protection activities by government do not pose a threat to private enterprise, as is sometimes alleged, for by and large those activities are designed—like a super Better Business Bureau with legal clout—to keep the "system" working. Drive the bad guys out: the basic businessmen are good, it's the few scoundrels who need to be controlled by public watchdogs!

The cooperator who is a thinking person sees that the cooperative system asks for neither the preservation of private profit nor for enlargement of government activity. Such a person sees cooperation as a well-rounded alternative philosophy, which is neither capitalist nor communist. Respecting the equal worth of all persons, the true cooperator craves a system which preserves the whole person, which allows for participation in those matters that concern him and his welfare, which is built around the needs and wants of the user. The system of thought represented by this cooperator says that, in the consumers' own businesses, the purpose is the service and not the exploitation of the consumer.

This view of cooperation is as American as apple pie, as old in our history as cooperative barn-raisings, as substantial as the mutual insurance systems envisaged and organized by Benjamin Franklin in the first days of the Republic. The development of large-scale capitalist and private empires, a latter-day development in the United States, has in no way diminished the enthusiasm for consumer and user ownership. The definitive historical works of Joseph Knapp,[1] the cooperative historian, clearly show that, since the beginning, the cooperative idea has been a strong factor in overall American development.

And Knapp is right. Look at some of the figures gathered by the Cooperative League of the USA. They reveal the strength of cooperative development. See facing page.

One person may belong to several cooperatives, of course. But there are still over fifty million memberships, fifty million decisions to belong to a cooperative organization. Included in that number are the recipients of service from cooperative banks, land-bank associations, production credit associations and cooperative or cooperative-oriented insurance companies. There is a significance in the totals: it is apparent that the cooperative idea works. Farmland Industries, Inc.,[2] a vast farmer-cooperative complex, working out of Kansas City, Missouri, is on the *Fortune* magazine's "Top 100" list, doing almost a billion dollars a year business for its members!

The point is that cooperation is not just a philosophy; it is a working system of doing business, one which has, in fact, eschewed dependence on the private-profit approach and which has not asked government to do the job.

Why can't we take this working system and apply it to our last rites? If the system works for all the other rites, why not the last ones? We have a right to our last rites; they belong to us more than they do to the private-profit funeral directors. If we can cooperate in providing those goods and services which give us life, which meet our needs, it is reasonable to expect that the philosophy and organizational system used by so many people can apply to our last request on earth: to die in dignity, to die in peace, to die solvent. We came into the world as the result of a cooperative act of procreation by our parents; surely it isn't unreasonable to have our last acts cooperative!

One could argue, of course, that, since the consumer is dependent on the business community and dependent on government already, the best thing to do would be to reform the business community and improve the quality of government. The response may rest in a combination of the idea that the consumer knows better what he needs and

Cooperative Facts and Figures, 1973

Kind of Co-op	Purpose	Number of Co-ops	Individual Members
Consumer goods centers	Food and home supplies	223	577,000
Credit unions	Thrift and credit	23,469	28,500,000
Electric co-ops	Rural electric service	996	6,266,815
Farm credit system			1 million
Banks for co-ops	Credit for co-ops	12	——
Federal land bank associations	Long-term farm credit	565	——
Production credit associations	Production credit	434	
Farm marketing supply and service	Higher returns	7,700	6,400,000
Fishing	Marketing supply, bargaining	90	10,000
Group health plans	Prepaid health care	100	5,000,000
Housing	Homes	800	500,000
Insurance, co-op oriented and mutual	Financial security	2,000	2,500,000
Memorial societies	Dignified last rites	120	600,000
Legal	Legal services	1,400	
Nursery schools	Preschool child care	1,600	60,000
Student co-ops	Bookstores and housing	338	20,000
Telephone co-ops	Rural telephone service	235	750,000

ought to do it himself and the idea that the best way for business and government to be reformed is to exercise our independence of it, or to show it yet better ways.

Help from Other Cooperators

Since there is so much cooperative experience, it would be reasonable to expect that cooperative organizations would have many people available to help our funeral cooperative get started. But that is not the case. There is helpful literature available. There are educational services available to local groups desiring to form cooperatives, but none of the national federations provides substantial help or expertise in organizing new groups. Their staffs are small, their assignments usually too great, for any staff member to do anything more than answer a letter. It is a rare event for a staff member to visit and to spend much time helping a group get on its way. When the movement talks about "self-help and mutual aid," or do-it-yourself, it really seems to mean it. That, of course, has its strengths.

From the standpoint of literature and ideas, the Cooperative League of the USA, a federation of cooperative organizations, is probably the most useful. From the standpoint of business organization, Universal Cooperatives, Inc.,[3] the central joint-buying group of United States cooperatives, probably has the most experience.

From the viewpoint of genuine concern and familiarity with the spirit of funeral reform, the Continental Association of Funeral and Memorial Societies is the paramount resource for people moving into the funeral field. Its focus, historically, has been on the memorial society. There are people in its constituency who are among the most knowledgeable in this country on what is wrong with today's funeral picture and what the alternatives are. Underfinanced, understaffed, its small office has too big a job to provide a local group with the benefits of its experience. However, it may know who might be helpful in your area.

It should be recognized that, despite the fact there are over one hundred memorial societies, there is relatively little experience with cooperative funeral homes. Morgan's *Manual* lists the following:

Winneshiek Co-op Burial Ass'n
Decorah, Ia. 52101

Eddyville Co-op Burial Ass'n,
Eddyville, Ia. 52553

Fremont Co-op Burial Ass'n
Fremont, Ia. 52561

Co-op Funeral Home,
Sioux Center, Ia. 51250

Benton & Adjoining Counties Co-op
Burial Ass'n,
Keystone, Ia. 52249

Garden Chapel Funeral Home
Pella, Ia. 50219

Sanborn Funeral Home, Box B,
Sanborn, Ia. 51248

Pella Co-op Funeral Home
Sully, Ia. 50251

Iowa State Federation of Co-op
Burial Assn's,
Reuben Schakel, Pres., Pella,
Ia. 50219

Freeborn County Funeral Ass'n,
Albert Lea, Minn. 56007

Northland Co-op Mortuary,
Cloquet, Minn. 55720

Sunset Burial Ass'n,
Echo, Minn.56237

Greenwood Prairie Burial Ass'n,
Elgin, Minn, 55932

Kandiyohi-Meeker Co-op Funeral
Ass'n,
Lake Lillian, Minn.56253

Tri-County Burial Ass'n,
Prinsburg, Minn. 56281

Range Funeral Home,
Virginia, Minn. 55792

Co-op Funeral Ass'n, 311 West Ave.
Talmadge, Ohio 44278

Minnehaha Funeral Home,
Baltic, S.D. 17003

Fraternal Burial Ass'n,
Viborg, S.D. 57070

Mesaba Funeral Chapel,
Hibbing, Minn. 55746

Reedsville Co-op Funeral Ass'n,
Reedsville, Wis. 54230

A basic principle is cooperation among cooperatives. Yet an organizer of a new group is not likely to find aggressive support from most societies, since they are usually preoccupied with the conduct of their own operations. On the basis of a survey request for basic information and attitudes from these cooperative funeral homes, the author believes that at least two are prepared to share experience, the Northland Chapel in Cloquet, Minnesota, whose president responded with interest to the idea of a book in the field, and the funeral homes associated with Range Cooperatives, in Virginia, Minnesota. Eli Ranta, general manager, said that "he would encourage development" in this field. Noting that "our prices average $200 to $300 less on every funeral than our competitors'," Ranta said that the group thus provides "a savings immediately plus the rebate at the end of the year." There may be individuals in the membership and on the staffs of the other societies who might respond to questions from a group desiring to organize a comparable facility.

Once in awhile, an all-round cooperative person appears on the scene, who will help anybody interested in organizing a cooperative. A man with such a reputation is Frank P. Anastasio, the executive director of Mid-Eastern Cooperatives,[4] located in Carlstadt, New Jersey. He is probably the best-known cooperative official in the northeast, with a growing national impact because of his substantial qualities. There are others like him throughout the country who, on their own time and out of their own interest, give long hours beyond the call of their own duties. Anastasio, responsible for a sizable cooperative food warehouse and bearing the incredible frustrations of a fast-growing field, has nevertheless given countless nights and days to helping new food-buying clubs, to giving priceless information to eager people who have searched for practical aid and guidance and found little until meeting Anastasio. Beginning as an accountant in a then small organization, Anastasio's twenty and more years have seen his own organization grow with his energy and grow with the times. Even with the added responsibilities that growth entailed, including a doubling of the size of the warehouse, he finds excitement in new and adventurous ideas, his mind sparkling with initiatives for the consumer. In the northeastern United States, he is a cooperative king-pin.

Because of pressure on his time and because of growing demands from largely urban groups in New York City, the cooperative leadership of Mid-Eastern organized several years ago a Council for Self-Help Development,[5] which is intended to help people find solutions to their problems through the use of the cooperative technique. It has its own staff man, the vigorous and effective John Gauci, but Anastasio, true to form, still finds himself on call.

There is another configuration of personalities, many new to cooperatives, who have brought into the movement skills and experience and attitudes of an entirely new generation. In the North American Student Cooperative Organization (NASCO),[6] proudly sub-titled Students of Cooperation, a vitality has been uncovered which speaks well for the movement's ability to attract reasonable and intelligent young people. In particular there are David McPhail Friedrichs, long-time NASCO coordinator, his associate Kathy McPhail Friedrichs, Margaret Lamb, a NASCO colleague, some of their associates in related groups, like John Achatz and Mary Farrell (all in Ann Arbor, Michigan), like Jay Jacob Wind (in Madison, Wisconsin), like Jim Jones (in East Lansing, Michigan).

While these people focus largely on student cooperatives, especially in housing, they have a universal dimension, a humane attractiveness, a sense of practical knowhow which help to get new programs started. The context is one of great faith.

Jack McLanahan is another good man. He and Connie, his partner, have been cooperators for the many years of their lifetime. Despite the analysis of a rigorous sociology that might discourage lesser persons, they see hope wherever they turn. Now presiding over a new idea, the Institute for a Democratic Economy[7] in Lansing, Michigan, the McLanahans are the kind of people who help other people, who opt for social invention, Old Believers who see the things that people should be doing for themselves.

The Thornthwaites of Detroit are another couple who have devoted their lives to cooperative activity. Fred, easily the most cantankerous and stubborn of all the cooperative administrators in the United States, balances those qualities with a rigorous faith and a direct humanity we need so desperately in movements for social change. Together, Fred and Virginia have influenced the lives of thousands of Detroit-area people, who have benefited from the optical centers, the housing centers, the contagious and creative spirit of Cooperative Services, Inc.[8]

There are older leaders too, whose experience is not being used at all or enough, retired from once powerful positions in the cooperative movement. Albert Marble, Eugene Mannila, Werner Regli, Robert Z. Willson, Jerry Voorhis, Leslie Woodcock, Eulah Feemster are vigorous people whose names come to mind easily.

Then there are the youthful believers like Stanley Yarkin of the Greenbelt, Maryland, complex of cooperatives. He has been an elected leader of the Cooperative Institute Association,[9] a conference-and-education organization whose potential, despite its forty-five years of existence, has not been recognized and used enough by the established cooperative movement. Nevertheless Yarkin continues to believe that even older, established organizations can help people stay alive intellectually. He practices a kind of pragmatic religion that one associates with the idea, "Keeping the faith." He follows in the path of Institute leader Aileen Paul of Leonia, New Jersey, who gave uncounted hours to the Institute, to keep it alive at its lowest hours. Through such beliefs and practices thousands of cooperators have demonstrated the vitality of the cooperative idea.

Some of these people are cooperators employed by their cooperatives; others are cooperators serving on their boards, loyal parts of the membership. It doesn't matter if they are on the staff or not, they will help if they can.

Another loyal and energetic person is Mary Jean McGrath of the University Center for Cooperatives[10] in Madison, Wisconsin. Her basic concerns as a warm and family-oriented person shine in her relationships with others. Her editorial work, her search for excellence, inspire those seeking the cooperative path. Don Rothenberg, new light in the Berkeley, California, cooperative group,[11] is the kind of person who talks to people in human terms. So is Max Awner, editor of that co-op's vibrant weekly. They are not merely professionals. They are cooperative persons and that is a difference. We have hired them because they are good.

Ed and Edna Turner, members of the Family Buying Cooperative Association,[12] devote many volunteer hours to their cooperative in Bayside, New York. In addition to the needs of a large family, they find time to help students at Queens College organize a Campus Cooperative Services organization, to help start a Queens College television program aimed at consumers; to organize a Queens Consumer Assembly[13] "for everyone." If there were a Cooperative Family of the Year, they would be among the prime nominees. The Turners are the kind of family around whom co-ops turn. They have their counterparts in hundreds of communities in the United States and Canada. "They will do anything for you if they can." You've heard that expression. Find those people to help.

Why this recitation of names and persons and jobs? The cooperative movement, of which Cooperative Funeral Homes are a part, is an ongoing cause that has attracted thousands upon thousands of truly high-quality people. It is not a bumptious Johnny-come-lately movement designed to save people from themselves, despite themselves.

People of substance and genuine concern, with lives of quality, with energy for good have found the movement attractive. It is why there will always be a cooperative movement, for as long as there are people such as these, they will seek better lives for themselves and their friends and neighbors. If there were no cooperative movement, these people would invent one, because their beliefs and practices lead them naturally and easily into self-help and mutual aid.

These unusual persons, these unusual organizations are the reason the cooperative movement is as strong as it is. It has captured the imagination of people who might have spent their lives in otherwise ordinary tasks but who, finding they could use their whole minds and lives, gave more than the ordinary. They have caught the charm and social significance of cooperation and, grateful for the gift of life they have received from it, return to it an unusual amount of devotion.

The same spirit is available to people desiring to organize Cooperative Funeral Homes. The social and business principles of cooperation, the sane common sense of good organization, are emphasized by these people. They are practical idealists. Those of us who plan new and relatively untried ventures should call on them and people like them to share the benefit of their experience, challenging them to help us apply in our settings the knowhow they have gathered in their cooperative pursuits.

I would not advocate calling up these people via long-distance telephone with the expectation of "instant cooperation." I mention them because of the quality of their lives and spirit, as typical of the kinds of persons in the cooperative movement who want to be helpful. They wake up in the mornings with headaches from time to time, too, and they argue with their partners. They get tired. They're human. They might turn you down. But the balance of their witness is helpfulness, and if they can't help, they may know people who will.

A Sense of History

The cooperative movement, in which Cooperative Funeral Homes will play a growing part, is not an accidental result of history. It is part of a self-conscious, consumer-oriented idea that people should have a larger say in their economic lives. The cooperative idea is today flourishing in many parts of the world, serving producers and consumers in substantial ways.

Out of the experience comes evaluation of performance and reevaluation of working principles. Historically, co-ops have relied on what have been called the Rochdale Principles, the methods of business used by those weavers in Rochdale, England, who in 1844 organized their own little food store as the opening wedge in a grand scheme for changing the world. Prior to that time, many co-op experiments had failed. But the weavers' principles seemed to work, leading to a worldwide movement of considerable influence.

Changing times produce new needs and new words. In an effort to define the working principles that seem to unite co-ops in the world today, the International Cooperative Alliance[14] outlined the essential ones as follows:

1. Open membership
2. One member, one vote
3. Limited or no return on share capital
4. Return to consumer use of any capital not risked
5. Continuous education

Acknowledging intercooperative mutual aid, the Alliance noted another principle:

6. All cooperative organizations, in order best to serve the interests of their members and their communities, should actively cooperate in every practical way with other cooperatives at local, national and international levels.

When a small group of persons in your community embarks on the drama of organizing consumers into a Cooperative Funeral Home, they are entering an international adventure. The Alliance commission that outlined today's operative principles noted that

Humanity at large is seeking, however blindly, for a major transformation from a system dominated by capital to one based on human dignity and equality. The Cooperative Movement, when true to its principles and armed with the courage of its convictions, can prove by practical demonstration that a world society is possible in which man is no longer the slave but the master of economic forces. Its mission is to teach the common people by demonstration how the principles which express their neighborly and brotherly relations in the economic cooperative can also inspire the mutual relations of the nations.

Every small cooperative, no matter the field of action, demonstrates the capacity of people to serve each other in a context of friendliness and human service. The Cooperative Funeral Home is one part of a large dream, an important part.

Won't Co-ops Fail?

The problem of failure plagues every effort by consumers who take up their own lives and try to order them in sensible, productive paths. Co-ops, like all human ventures, fail. But a new look at failure may be needed: if a co-op lasts for six months or a year or two only, for that period of time it was a success, it was doing its job, it gave its participants a glimpse of a better way of doing things.

The possible failure of co-ops needs to be matched against the chronic failure of private-profit businesses and government to meet the needs of the consumer. They fail all the time; they have rarely succeeded. What has kept these failures in operation is the lack of experience and will among consumers to organize their own lives themselves and provide themselves with the goods and services they need. All else having failed, consumer cooperation needs a hearty try by all concerned. The penalty for not trying is continuing dependence on institutions that have amply demonstrated their incapacity.

Let consumers do their own thing!

The Day-to-Day Business

7

People mistakenly call cooperatives nonprofit. Most conventional ones are not. They are business organizations that make profits, which are earnings or income of the business in excess of the amount needed for the maintenance of the property, taxes—all of its bills—the salaries, some reserves, and so on. They differ from the private-profit business in that the profits are returned to the member-user in proportion to that person's patronage of the business.

An organizing committee will have to consult the laws of its state, since laws differ widely in their handling of cooperative organizations. Because of the uniqueness of Cooperative Funeral Homes, it is probably wise to consult, or have your friendly participating lawyer consult, your state's attorney general and, possibly, the division of state government responsible for supervising the funeral industry in your state. Such consultation, ahead of time, is time well spent. It is better to have knowing and understanding consent early than probing uncertainty later.

The organizing committee should have little difficulty pursuing the proper incorporation procedure. (It is possible that the memorial society's initial incorporation papers permit the ownership and operation of funeral facilities, and it is worth checking out.) There may be some minor resistance, particularly if there is no Cooperative Funeral Home in your state.

Dr. Hollis S. Ingraham, commissioner of health for New York State, whose agency supervises the funeral industry, asked by a reporter for the Rockland County, New York, *Journal-News* about the question of cooperative ownership, is quoted as saying, "The economic or commercial aspects of such a plan would not fall within our area of responsibility. We would have no quarrel with such a group, providing it could meet the funeral licensing laws of New York State."

That attitude is likely to be the open attitude of most administrators. After all, if the larger and posher funeral homes in New York City can be owned by a large out-of-state corporation solely for investment reasons, as they are, there is certainly no reason why a group of citizens cannot own and operate a local facility for their mutual benefit.

The Direct-Charge System

Some pioneers in the future will wish to explore application of the "direct-charge" idea in the Cooperative Funeral Home setting. Because of the newness of this cooperative variant, it is probably wise to approach cooperative organization from the more conventional standpoint, though a basic outline of direct charge is offered here for those who might wish to consider it in the very beginning.

Basically, the direct-charge approach deals with the questions of profit by eliminating it. Consumers worry about profits. Even in some of the larger conventional cooperatives there is a lurking fear among some members that someone, somewhere, is "making a buck," gathering in the profits. The direct-charge cooperative charges the member-consumer for the services rendered or the goods provided just what they cost. (In a food setting, the price to the consumer is the wholesale cost paid by the cooperative.)

But, you ask quite properly, what about the cost of electricity, the cost of leasing or maintaining facilities—the necessary items of normal overhead? In the direct-charge food cooperative, such costs are divided among the members, who agree in contract to pay their share of the maintenance costs, usually on a weekly basis. This may be 75 cents; it may be more or less, depending on the capacity of the members to keep down costs through voluntary labor, through self-service techniques (such as marking the prices on your own commodities), through expecting less. The 75-cent figure, if that is what it takes to operate the facility, is evaluated in terms of its adequacy at quarterly meetings of the membership, who agree to change the figure if costs change. It is a fascinating and welcome innovation in social pioneering, for it deals with the lingering capitalist uncertainty which rides into the cooperative system: How much profit is right profit? What is a fair charge? And all the rest. Profit as a *problem* is removed from the scene.

Instantly, the observer will see the difficulty in its application in the Cooperative Funeral Home. The member will not use the services each year. In the food field, the consumer approaches his marketplace with regularity. Would the funeral consumer-member consent to sharing costs of operation if he has no use for the services for years and years? (However, if there are enough members, it is conceivable that an annual cost-of-operation fee, divided among themselves, might be acceptable. People pay $5 and $10 to valued associations all the time, why not to practical social programs?)

The direct-charge *principle* might be used in auto repair shops, appliance centers and a dozen other places as well as funeral homes. The creative and practical people in your organizing group should explore the implications of the following: when the consumer-member comes to the Cooperative Funeral Home to make arrangements for a funeral, he will be charged the actual cost of services and merchandise for which he contracts. Every purchase of merchandise would be sold at cost. The consumer-member can check the invoices, if he has any doubts. He will also be charged for the cost of labor, in terms of actual time spent by the funeral house employees. If an employee is receiving $5 an hour, $7.50 an hour or more, that will be the charge passed along to the consumer. Fair enough: direct charge is the guiding principle.

What about the costs of operation, however? A sound enterprise will have an educated guess about such costs over a period of time, an estimate on expenses. For a new organization, such calculations are inherently more difficult, of course, but such projections are necessary. The key element in the accounting is the number of funerals the Cooperative Funeral Home will conduct, can conduct in terms of its physical and manpower limitations. It is wiser to plan lower numbers than higher. The planners will need to divide the cost of operations by the number of funerals to find the cost of operations per funeral. Other variants for accounting will develop with experience, of course. A noticeably different element in the funeral home situation is that the calculated costs of operation will have to include the "idle time" of employees, though in the kind of Cooperative Funeral Home we would wish to conduct, such employees might well become engaged in the valuable educational and teaching and public relations activities of the organization. No time should be wasted. Quarterly calculations of correct charges for costs of operation will be necessary, with suitable revisions. Any excess earnings, beyond actual expenses of operation, can be used either to reduce the costs per user during the next quarter or used for special expansion or educational funds.

The system is unique, and a group is well advised to explore applications with experienced people in the direct charge field.[1]

The Usual Cooperative System

Using traditional systems of doing cooperative business will appeal more readily to most organizers, because they are more familiar. Basically, the fee approach would be to evaluate total costs of the institution, charging enough per funeral to pay for costs of merchandise, labor used and enough excess to allow for a slow business period. Profits earned (money that was not needed to provide the services, conduct the business, set enough aside for reserves) can be returned to that year's users, in the form of rebates, the amount calculated on the dollar-value of the purchases made. An experienced accountant on your organizing committee can help with the calculations.

Part of the profits may also be distributed among those people who have invested more than just their membership contribution to the organization. Building funds, expansion funds and similar capital programs are often financed through membership contributions, and modest dividends for such confidence are probably in order.

The key to the cooperative system is the member. The body of the society is its members. Members meet annually for an overall review of the business, to elect members to the board of directors, to hear reports from management, to exercise their fundamental rights as owners of the business. They can meet twice a year, but an annual meeting is customary.

The board of directors conducts the affairs of the cooperative between annual meetings. It is entrusted with considerable responsibility, but it is always accountable to the membership. Its rights are only those granted them by the membership: no more and no less. The members of the board need to be allowed to use their intelligence, their good sense of the rightness and fitness of things and to make decisions.

One of the main responsibilities of a board of directors, operating under the mandates provided by the general membership, is the hiring of staff. The usual approach is that the board will interview persons for the post of manager, depending on him to hire others he needs to conduct the business properly. The manager is responsible to the board.

It is essential that the board understand its proper functions in relation to a hired manager. The board is responsible for the development of basic policy: what shall be done, its spirit, its intent. The manager is responsible for the administration of such policies, for recommending new ones and modifications as experience suggests.

Two problems arise out of such simple formulations. One is that board members, naturally interested in the success of the organization, might dabble in the affairs of the business. They should not. Such practice can contribute to bad morale. When board members interfere with the conduct of business, giving their own instructions to personnel and so on, they are getting in the way of the natural flow of leadership from the manager to *his* staff. If a board member has suggestions or advice, he can offer it at a board meeting, which is normally attended by the manager. When a director or any co-op member takes a volunteer post within the business establishment itself, the wiser course is for that person to be responsible to the manager, as if he were a paid staff member.

While interfering with the manager is a serious problem and reflects bad board/management philosophy, perhaps the most destructive, from the cooperative point of view, occurs when the board withdraws from its natural function of linking membership needs with management operations and lets the manager take over the business. Many large cooperative organizations suffer from the dangers offered by otherwise-competent management. Under such circumstances, the board counsels less frequently, takes less responsibility for policy. The manager begins to talk about and think about the board as "*my* board*.*" Many stalwart cooperative men and women have left the movement discouraged, because of what they call the professional takeover, the assumption of power and authority by elitist management groups whose concern becomes less the welfare of the membership and the engagement of the membership in its own welfare than the preservation of the prerogatives and tenure-in-office of the management group.

The Cooperative Funeral Home can be kept cooperative by focusing constantly on the membership, who are the seat of power, the reason for being, the actual constituency of the organization. The organization does not exist for the management, it does not exist for the board: it exists for its members and its members alone. A sharp eye must be kept on the democracy of cooperatives. Unless wary of the intrusion of well-meaning elitists (who think they know better than consumers what consumers need and want), co-ops will be cooperative in legal form only but not in spirit or action.

The interim board takes the first steps, makes fundamental arrangements, functions in trust. It is building for the future membership. It is not building a permanent empire for itself but an organization, whose first annual meeting of members will elect a continuing board of directors. The right spirit of work is central to the success of cooperative operations. The board, composed of volunteers, must preserve the democratic idea, always checking back to the central proposition: the purpose of the cooperative is the service of the membership.

Long-Range Planning

All planning by an interim board is long-range planning, of course. But some functions are immediate, others are in the future. It is considered a good use of everyone's time if a working board divide up its functions between its regular meetings, so that particular problems can be analyzed in detail and particular skills and interests of board members used to the maximum.

One important committee can deal with long-range planning. This is the group that helps to set the stage into which the separate parts will fit and act. In some cases the competencies of an entire board can be combined into a committee of the whole which absorbs all the functions of otherwise separate committees—but most people on boards prefer not to be active at *all* levels. They may prefer instead to hear committee reports and recommendations when the entire board meets, then react to them, approving them after discussion and the chance to contribute comments and additions have been provided.

The long-range planning committee is a natural repository for exploration about property needs, about the overall investment needs of the organization, consideration of zoning and other questions related to the operation of facilities, the exploration of possible sites, decisions about renting/leasing/owning/building property. This group must calculate the amount of capital that will have to be raised among the membership through gifts or loans (the latter more likely) and from commercial or cooperative lending institutions. The cost of repaying money, rented from the members or from lending institutions, is a part of the cost of doing business and must be kept in mind in overall budget-making.

Just what does it cost to set up a cooperative funeral business? Estimates range from $50,000 to $100,000. Much depends on the tastes of the seekers. A fancy baronial mansion is one thing; a modest usable facility is another. Buying existing buildings and building new ones inject another element. The choice between renting and owning is important: some groups will prefer to lease for a few years, moving into ownership and all its responsibilities at a later time when the future of the business can be assessed more realistically.

The cost of equipment within the selected structure is a capital question. Not only is the technical equipment in the semimedical "operating room" costly, but there is the matter of furnishings for the entire house. Chairs, sofas for sitting areas, drapes, carpets and the other accoutrements of an attractive establishment must be accounted for. Is all of this available in used condition, from funeral directors going out of business? Must new equipment be purchased? Is it more economical to buy new, in the long run, since breakdowns will be fewer and replacement needs not so immediate? A supply of variously priced caskets will have to be provided also.

The long-range planning committee can also look at the overall ratio of consumers served to staff and other needs. Basically, it can create a five-year or ten-year master plan, which will show its growth from stage to stage. A master plan can acknowledge the transition from rented to owned facilities; it can acknowledge goals for membership recruitment and growth; it can evaluate work-load to staff requirements.

There is no reason why the long-range planning committee should not draw on the experience and insight of those experienced funeral directors who form the teaching staffs of the colleges of mortuary science, attended by future funeral directors. Such consultations, free or at a charge, are valuable and should be sought. A planning group may also have the benefit of a friendly and interested practicing funeral director, perhaps from the immediate community and more likely from a distant one. A good adviser might very well be hopeful of becoming the manager of such a group and will offer good advice, knowing he/she might be invited to serve the group at a decent salary in a decent environment dedicated to service and not profits. There is also no reason why the Funeral Directing Bureau (or whatever the state's regulatory commission is called) and its staff should not be called on to advise. You would not wish to interfere with the proper administration of funeral law in your state: you are well advised, as they are, to think through all kinds of problems ahead of time. Such official groups have the duty to help serious cooperators about to organize a business. That must be our assumption. It does their own industry little good to have agencies of the state oppose cooperative effort simply because all or most of the business to date has been private-profit rather than social-gain motivated. Their job, even though the commissioners are usually funeral directors, is to advise, supervise and guide the *entire* industry through the proper uses and respect of funeral law. In these days of consumer consciousness, it ill behooves public agencies and trade associations themselves to discriminate against consumer agencies. Consumer groups should move fearlessly into every arena, seeking advice, asking questions, assuming the best.

Long-range planning is long-range dreaming. The committee mixes its visions with a firm reality, based on an assessment of the growth of the business, its financial needs and probable stresses.

Buying Out an Established Business

Private-profit funeral directors buy out established businesses. Sometimes funeral directors die (too!) and their business and good will are on the market to the highest bidder. When you see a funeral directing company grow from one to two to three and more outlets, it has sometimes come about through the addition of established businesses. The owner of a business wants to fly to Florida with his wife: he's made enough money to retire. If he can sell his business, he'll have even more money.

The use of the good will of a respected local name for a Cooperative Funeral Home is worth considering, if the man will sell the business to you and if the respect he has is deserved. But it may be hard to persuade the public that the Jones Funeral Home, now under the management of a cooperative, is different. If you change the name to the Spring Valley Cooperative Funeral Home, then you're buying physical location, equipment and supplies, but not the good will.

The choice should be considered and not rejected out of hand. However, weight should be given to the view that a brand-new approach, an entirely different kind and quality of funeral home might deserve a brand-new image of its own, one not touched by the earlier presence of the typical funeral home on the typical spot on typical Main Street. If it is an established business become cooperative, the passing public might not even notice the change: the house will look the same, the sign will be at the same spot, the aura is the same. Some new marks, some new signs, a new house-painting may be in order to develop new visions, new allegiance, an impression of genuine difference.

Physical Needs

Pity the Cooperative Funeral Home on crowded Main Street, where attenders at funeral occasions have to vie for parking spaces with shoppers at the supermarket and the local movie house. Parking is essential. A large municipal lot nearby is an asset, private parking with enough car space a distinct advantage.

The typical Cooperative Funeral Home will not be much different from the private-profit Home in facilities. There will be a lobby; there will be adaptable rooms, large and small enough for the varying-size funeral occasions that will be required. There needs to be a display room for the various kinds of coffins (all right, caskets) that may be made available, with clearly marked prices on all of them. Clothing, should it be desired, will have to be displayed in an appropriate place. There need to be the necessary workrooms for the funeral director and his staff, where bodies can be held awaiting decision-making by the family, kept for transportation instructions or cosmetically prepared for open-casket display if that is required by the survivors. There need to be some rooms for memorial meetings and related occasions. If the body is to be displayed, or if the closed casket is to be at the center of a floral display or if a memorial meeting is to be held (with the body long-since disposed of), then space of varying dimensions is needed. Ideally, one occasion ought not to interfere with another. Consumers deserve choice; they also deserve privacy. The sound of music from a crowded memorial meeting from which gentle laughter may spring occasionally ought not to interfere with the private prayers of a devout family before the coffin of its deceased father. A family should be helped to follow its chosen path, its own way.

This dimension—this need for choice—is an extra problem for Cooperative Funeral Home organizers. In addition to the above needs, there must be room for educational gatherings, for meetings of the board of directors. Many spaces are adaptable and will have two or three uses: they just must be kept in mind! While the Cooperative Funeral Home performs the usual services of the typical Home, it has a social dimension with new requirements. With an emphasis on lower cost funerals—and a willing membership to go along with it—less display space is needed for the more splendid caskets. Some buying, indeed, might even be by catalog if the wholesale supplier is nearby. With more space available, the social purposes of the institution can be maximized. (Most people do not appreciate looking at caskets, anyway, finding it a most unpleasant task—leading to a hurried and usually expensive purchase.)

Hiring a Funeral Director

It would be ideal for a Cooperative Funeral Home to discover a student in a College of Mortuary Science who is interested in service in a not-for-profit organization. While the student completes the education usually required for licensing, the Home could be completing its own arrangements. Unfortunately, the atmosphere of the field reduces that possibility to a relatively small group. Students are attracted by potentially high income, by the uniqueness and prestige of the field; few move into it as a way to serve people. If such a student can be found, be thankful.

Many funeral directors, working for established private-profit funeral houses, are on salary. There is no reason why a cooperatively owned Home could not draw on that reservoir of people, many of whom lack capital to begin their own place and prefer to rely instead on the owner's assumption of risk.

A College of Mortuary Science is likely to help its graduates find employment; its director should be consulted. Many students are not interested in the details of ownership. They merely want to work in the field at a decent salary.

On the other hand, the difficulty with a recent student is that he is not likely to have the kind of business experience an established director can offer. The board of directors of the cooperative might happen to include persons with such insight and the problem is solved. If no one has the experience, it is wise to seek out an experienced person—who may be looking for a change, who may not like working conditions in the place where he is currently employed, who would rather be a bigger cog in a smaller wheel than a small cog in a large wheel.

What does the Cooperative Funeral Home have to offer a licensed funeral director?

1. As stated earlier, the cooperative offers a funeral director an opportunity to work in the chosen field without the responsibilities of ownership.

2. The cooperative offers a humane and warm atmosphere in which to work, an environment of service.

3. The cooperative offers an opportunity for a person to excel in the chosen field; good salesmanship is not a criterion for professional and financial growth in the cooperative.

4. The cooperative offers a funeral director a social incentive, for its service motivations are genuine.

5. The cooperative offers a funeral director an opportunity to work in a pioneering setting, to have pride in contributing to a new field: consumer ownership of a basic community service.

6. The cooperative offers a funeral director a salary commensurate with his contribution: cooperatives in most fields offer salaries suitable to the particular area of enterprise. The cooperative offers psychic income, too, which cannot be measured so easily.

7. The cooperative offers a funeral director concern about his welfare, family, conditions of life: it is not interested in exploiting him for the sake of its members. He can expect to work hard, do a decent piece of work and be treated as a human being should be treated by employers: fairly, responsibly, with concern.

8. The cooperative offers a funeral director an opportunity to use his educational and organizational skills to good effect. Tasks other than those merely "required" will fill the director's mind and time, as he participates in a program of community education that would be expected of a cooperative in this field. The director can be the all-round person and worker he always wanted to be.

If the cooperative finds a funeral director with some experience, its personnel committee will have to accept one task: the retraining of that individual.

It is a big leap for an employee to switch from a private-profit establishment to a cooperative one. Cooperative supermarkets, for example, in New York City and elsewhere acknowledge the need for retraining: a butcher or delicatessen worker may be so accustomed to cheating on weights, to "adding his thumb" to the scales that he must be re-oriented by the cooperative or re-orient himself completely. Cooperative auto repair shops and service stations have the identical problem. An employee in a private-profit framework often learns to cheat the consumer: it is a part of the process of doing business. He must wink at irregularities, he must not criticize from a social perspective his employer's practices and decisions, he may be called upon to participate in outright skullduggery and must do so in order to keep his job. The private profit style has demoralized millions of people who, taught to do good at mother's knee, in church and in school, becoming eager to serve, find they are in conflict with business standards when they go to work.

A new employee needs to be tenderly supervised. The problem of old attitudes needs to be acknowledged and thoroughly discussed: a board of directors would be derelict in its duty if it failed to reeducate its new employees. All the valuable and meaningful organizational and educational work of months and years can be destroyed in a few weeks of old-style performance by an untrained employee.

Once the Home is in operation, if an existing employee has sufficient experience to become the manager, the duty of transforming old-idea employees into new-idea ones can be partly his and partly the personnel committee's.

The background for such reorientation is in the board of directors. It must know what it wants. It may be better not to open the Home or to delay its opening than to open with the wrong employees. The employee, after all, is the front line of the cooperative organization. Most co-op members have more contact with employees than with elected board members, thus their quality is vital to the co-op.

"What do we want in an employee?" A Home's eagerness to begin operation should not overcome the importance of answering that question; let it take weeks, if necessary. The cooperative will rise and fall on the answer. A job description should be the result of such discussions, one which can be given to a prospective employee and which can serve as a continuing point of reference and renewal as the cooperative grows.

Role of Members: Annual Meeting

The annual meeting of members is the prime official contact of the member with his cooperative. Members should meet. They must meet. Some cooperatives, eager to maintain contact with members, arrange for half-yearly meetings as well. A cooperative out of touch with its members is dead. Members who let the cooperative function without them contribute to the loss of psychic capital that is a cooperative's main asset.

The annual meeting gives the board of directors an opportunity to report on its care of the cooperative since the last meeting. Every phase of the cooperative's operations should be discussed openly with the members: it is their cooperative. Finances, long-range problems and plans, educational activities, reports of committees, property committee, staff report: everything belongs to the members. All information belongs to the members. Members must approve or disapprove the directions of the cooperative.

There may be recommendations from the board to the membership for consideration and perhaps, if the time is right, for approval.

A vital part of the usual annual meeting is the election or reelection of directors. The By-laws should require that the board be organized in such a way as to permit a healthful change of some directors every year. Co-ops can die if board incest occurs: the reappointment of directors year after year. Such in-breeding kills the participatory spirit: board membership is the best way to acknowledge the usefulness and interest of particular members, it is the best way to keep the organization alive and hopping with new ideas and new spirit, it is the best way to build, over a period of time, an informed and articulate membership. Few people are so critical to the success of a co-op organization that they must be reappointed year after year; no co-op should lean so much on any individual. A cooperative enterprise should be so well organized that many members will have acquired sufficient skill, interest and enterprise to fill the boots of anyone, should death or circumstances cause the dropping-out of a person. In any event, no one person should hoard skills and knowledge in his head.

Retiring directors should be sincerely thanked for their stint in office. The distribution of plaques and wall-hangings and silver cups, the conduct of testimonial dinners, are a false and costly use of resources. A hearty and honest public thank-you should be enough for a sincere cooperator; that person knows he gained as much as he gave. He might instead wish to thank the organization for the privilege of service! These comments, as well as others, will need modification to suit the particular slant, experience and orientation of local groups: they may be too idealistic for most people, and not sufficiently realistic. If you *have* to give a silver cup or a thank-you dinner, do so.

To be utterly realistic (and sometimes it hurts), unless members are fully imbued with the excitement of their cooperative, they are not likely to rush to the annual meeting of a Cooperative Funeral Home. Many members would just as soon forget about the business of their own organization. Sometimes, however, moving beyond the conduct of necessary business can generate greater participation: a debate on current issues in the funeral field, a dinner just before the business meeting, a visiting lecturer, a musician, a theater experience offered by a local group might tip the scales for an individual wondering whether or not to attend. No matter what the level of participation by members may be, organizers should not be disappointed: even absent members are appreciative of their cooperative. That's why they joined. They share in its benefits; they know why it exists; they probably "sell" the idea to visitors to their home. Sometimes organizations lay too much guilt on "no-shows." It is not necessary. Just do the best you can. Those who were absent can read all about the event in the newsletter.

Role of Members: The Social Service Committee

Not everyone can serve on the board of directors. Many people can put their talent and interest to work on committees of the membership which focus on narrower concerns. Sometimes committee life can be so interesting and exciting that people prefer it to the overall attention to the affairs of the business that must be provided at the board level. The chairmen of committees can meet with the board, too, communicating experience and conclusions to the board, maintaining the essential links to a co-op that, when neglected, become divisive.

A social service committee is fundamental to a consumer-owned facility. Sensitive to the strains that accompany a family at the time of a funeral, this committee can plan, supervise and conduct an ongoing program of caring. In the private-profit setting, the funeral director's concern ends when the last member of the funeral party has left, the bills have been paid and the limousines are all safely parked and gassed for their next use. This businesslike coolness is not appropriate to a consumer operation, whose very commitment is to the membership's needs. Consumers want more from their own operation and they should receive it.

What do consumers want and what should a social service committee do? And why is a social service committee needed? (Local organizers may differ with the author on this and other perspectives: variety will spice our cooperative life.)

Consumers are weary of being treated as objects of commerce whose only role is to provide a fishing pond for the profit-seekers. New institutions, which they create for themselves, support themselves, will provide the kind of service now resting only in our science-fiction minds, but which will become reality as we acquire more and more experience in many fields of endeavor.

In Chapter 9 there is a review of variants that make sense in a consumer-oriented society. But the base, before they can be considered, is required. The logic of consumer demands would suggest the wisdom of a social service committee as central to the heart-throb of a new-type Cooperative Funeral Home.

The social service committee, as a minimum task, will learn that death plays a powerfully disturbing role in a consumer family. No matter how sophisticated the family, no matter how much planning had occurred, no matter how lingering the illness of the deceased (with the time that may permit to think about the inevitability of death), death comes as a blow. It should be the task of the social service committee to do what the larger family and oldtime neighborhood did. Of course, many communities still do rise to meet the needs of a family in distress, and in that situation other tasks will be performed by the committee. If we are a community of people, centered on the matter of death, we should function as a community in whatever ways are needed. That means meals for the family, arrangements for baby-sitting, assistance with form-filling-out, letters to Social Security and benevolent societies and trade unions for death benefits. That means making telephone calls to distant relatives and friends, being with the survivors and on call, it means helping with the details of arrangements if help is needed. It might mean sleeping-in for a day or two. It might mean weeks of dropping in, just to see that "everything's all right."

Busybodies we don't need. Everyone will agree to that. But friends we do need. And a social service committee can be that kind of friend, sensitive, available, listening, alert.

If energy and concern and a genuine forward-looking directness are available in the people your Cooperative Funeral Home attracts, a truly different kind of social service may grow, a ministry prepared for anything. There is the possibility that saddened lives may need help, that families may need reorganization, that life-adjustments and moves to distant parts are called for: the ideal is that a Cooperative Funeral Home will stay with the family's survivors, in every respect, until the pieces of a new life are pulled together and there is a mutual sense that the help is no longer needed. Isn't that what friends are for?

Widows and widowers speak of the deep loneliness that strikes. Friends have returned to their normal routines. The children have boarded planes to distant cities and their own immediate families. The widow or the widower stands alone, more alone than experience has ever provided in a long life. If the social service committee is alert, is manned by the right kind of people, the loneliness following death (which must be accepted, of course) will be balanced by opportunities for new living, new activities, new sharing.

It is a strange fact of life that friends sometimes find it difficult to visit the lone survivor. We always thought of visiting two people. What will we talk about? Will we always talk about the deceased partner? Will there always be sadness? We're afraid we'll slip and ask, "How's Charlie?" when we are in a relaxed mood. Times are hard not only for survivors but for friends as well. A social service committee will study the phenomenon of death and the reactions of people to it and will know what is happening. Fine books are available to help members of the committee.[2] If the cooperative includes thoughtful psychologists, clergy with training in counseling, wise senior citizens, they might be induced to serve. The committee, in any event, should know all the resources of the community, so that if professional help is needed, the right connections can be made. The committee is a link, in all its activities, to help, to friendships, to a new life. That is social service. We could expect it only from a cooperative. It would be unreasonable to expect it from a private-profit funeral establishment.

Whether plans were laid ahead of time or are made at the time of death, not all people will function as calmly and as coolly as the two survivors whose telephone conversations we overheard in Chapter 4. The conversations sounded controlled, in any event, and we do not know the stresses the people may have been feeling. If their emotions had been clearly evident to Tim Jones, our funeral director, his service role would have been no different.

One of the wheels Tim set into motion in both cases was the hospitality wheel. The same social service committee included in its membership yet others who were alerted to a death: the counselors. Tim told Art Bleem, the head counselor and a psychologist, of the death and gave his own impressions of the condition of the person who called. (If someone had called for the survivor, Tim would have inquired into the survivor's condition.) The counselor and his colleagues then decided how to proceed.

The counselors take for granted feelings of grief and guilt among the survivors. It is a universal condition. Some show it clearly, others hold it in. Death mounts to a rousing crescendo the little submerged feelings of inadequacy and incompleteness everyone has when he thinks of his primary relationships. No relationships are so perfect and so complete that they exclude regret over uncompleted plans, sorrow over bad times of the past, feelings that maybe if more of this and that had been done the deceased's life would have been happier. Survivors may even feel responsibility for the death of their loved one, out of circumstances immediately preceding the death. Should the doctor have been called earlier? "Amy had complained about a headache, but I didn't pay any attention."

Members of the co-op know about the volunteer counselors. They will not be surprised at a telephone call and a visit at the door. It will be understood that the counselors function in confidence.

A quiet cry maybe. Acknowledgment of private fears and worries. A difficult but necessary phone call thought through out loud. An embrace of reassurance. Some discussion of the future. Sell the house? What do I do now? The reordering of the pace of a life accustomed to another begins slowly. The counselor responds. The counselor is an official friend, an ombudsman, a minister, a navigator through emotional shoals who will stay close to survivors in the first days. A phone call. A quick drop-in visit. Arrangement for the survivor to sleep at a friend's house, if that seems in order.

The social service committee, in this sense, institutionalizes what a community ought to do, perhaps once did but does no longer. It is the community wrapping its arms around the survivor, giving love in the visible form that means so much when the mind is filled only with loss. Oh, don't institutionalize, some will protest, there's too much organization anyway. In the field of death—as with most serious problems —the tendency among most of us is to run away from the situation and not toward it. To respond to death by moving toward the troubled circle is to think about death, and many people wish to set that aside "for now." The sharing of responsibility, the recognition of the role of friends and counselors, is as good for the co-op and its people as it is for the recipient.

Some people will not wish the help of the social service committee. Their friends may be adequate enough. They themselves may be strong enough to handle all the arrangements. People vary. Some will want to be left alone. A good friend such as the committee wants to know that, anyway. The availability of help and caring sometimes means more than the acts themselves, just to know that someone out there is on call if the spirit declines and the body is weary of responsibilities at the time of death of a loved one.

Through educational occasions, seminars and discussions, the handling of grief and guilt will become a familiar task to many co-op members, as they recognize their role in a community. It will not be a matter for paid professionals alone. It will be self-help and mutual aid at life's severest time. Those with responsibility on the social service committee, sensitive and alert as they are, will learn to know when a particular problem is beyond their capacity and they will know whom to call in on particular crises, which might be deeply psychological, medical or both. A favored clergyman, a friend of the survivor's, may not know of the distress of his parishioner; the survivor may even be reluctant to call on him. The committee can make that connection.

It is a wise and beautiful system, which, built into the life of the Cooperative Funeral Home, will spin new webs of relationship in communities torn apart now by the isolation of little residential plots, regional and district schools, social, economic and racial stratifications. What emerges as response to basic human need lasts beyond the immediate need. A community's life is slowly rebuilt by attitudes and actual experiences of caring, by the renewed or new perception of people as neighbors and friends, "as human and as real as I am."

Much of the underlying emotion at funeral time is deeply rooted. It needs to be expressed. The formalized weeping procedures of some traditions have enabled many of that tradition's people to free themselves of their inner emotions through external and publicly accepted acts. Some people, from other traditions, have difficulty with the expression of emotion. The emotion is there, nevertheless, and needs help. What can be done?

A counselor may have acquired, either through his own training or through learning experiences provided by the cooperative, useful patterns of counseling techniques. As counselor, known as counselor, the friendly visitor may occasion by his very presence expressions of emotion. It is good to encourage crying. One school of experience, identified as Re-Evaluation Counselling,[3] may provide a useful tool for counselors. Through the co-counseling approach, the counselor listens (within the structure encouraged by the "R.C." movement) to his "client," and then the "client" becomes the "counselor" for the other. It is a shared release of feelings. Analysis as such is absent from such a thoughtful and profound session; only release of pent-up feelings and the redirection of thought by the "client" himself are present. Training is required for this lay approach, which has not yet been used widely within the context of death experience, but with the growth of Cooperative Funeral Homes (and their service structures) may well come a natural search for new and effective methods of dealing with grief and guilt. "R.C." may be one of them.

There has been a decline of faith in the human capacity of individuals. Professionalization of the simplest services has denuded the citizen of his warmest clothing: the power to help others. Traveler's Aid, Red Cross, Blood Bank, Mental Health clinics and the like, while understandable in the context of the need for serious, organized help, have caused harm. Shall we say to the genuinely hungry beggar: "Find Traveler's Aid"? Or to the automobile accident victim, we the only observer, "I cannot help you—help is on the way"?

The Cooperative Funeral Home democratizes the specialties, restoring them to where they were, returning them to the person who never should have relinquished the desire to help in the first place. Where is it written that persons shall not help each other in times of mourning? It is written that we should. Too often we stand around, waiting for someone else to act. It has happened in the funeral field, as it has happened elsewhere. It need not continue. We need to build that sense of self-confidence that was taken away from us the first time that the blacksmith or the barber said he would take on the functions of arranging for the burials in his town.

The civilization of grief was a mistake. The people who weep and wail are right. They embarrass the cool citizens among us, but the deep recesses of our collective mind leading to loud demonstrations of distress are instinctively sounder than the views of those who proclaim the indignity of public tears. There are signs of growing wisdom in these matters, as people discover and rediscover patterns of thought and study that recognize the importance of emotional well-being through the uses of emotion. Men may cry, once again, joining psychologically more advanced women, who until now cried for both. Weeping and wailing and gnashing of teeth (what an old image!) belong to the people.

An educated staff, board and membership of the Cooperative Funeral Home, through study, sharing and experience, will become skilled in the problems and emotions related to death.

On Education

Another important member activity is the education committee. This is the committee that keeps the cooperative idea alive, by helping members keep in touch with the organization's essential difference: it is a co-op. This committee tries to help every member be aware what a co-op is: it is not just competing with private-profit funeral parlors, it is different in that people are working together for their mutual benefit.

This committee can be responsible for a newsletter designed to reach all members, interested community people, the media and the heads of sympathetic organizations. Its regular appearance, if only twice a year, keeps the co-op in the consciousness of the community. A simple but well-done mimeographed sheet is enough and, if budget allows, more expensive printing can be used. The point is communication. The newsletter can welcome new members, report committee work and recommendations, introduce new volunteers and staff members, include a report from the manager, provide ongoing financial statistics, review new literature in the funeral field, conduct an exchange of correspondence, answer "questions frequently asked." More often than not, a well-thought-through newsletter is likely to be handed by a member to a friend: it has many uses!

This committee can also conduct special meetings throughout the year, organize debates, provide an occasion for clarification of thought. It can issue posters for organizational bulletin boards, exhibits and displays for schools and libraries, literature for literature racks. This is the group that is entrusted with the noblest of tasks, the gentle persuasion of minds.

This committee and all committees should have a stated assignment. Things always work out better when people know what they are supposed to do. And then also you have a basis for accountability. "Who's doing what" is information more important than people realize: it keeps the co-op on the move.

Membership Gathering

Unless a decision has been made to incorporate the functions of membership gathering and recording in the frame of the education committee, there is a justifiable separate life for such a membership committee. Membership gathering is as vital as oats to a horse. It is the life of the new community you are building: to ignore it is to dry up the most essential resource of all. There is often an early excitement which produces new members, but the process must continue for the life of the cooperative. Many groups have grown old, riding on the needs and fortunes of the first handful. The cause of funeral reform is too important: younger families and persons must be fed into the membership constantly.

This group can audit welcoming procedures, being certain that proper attitude and service are provided. Do members have suggestions to make? The feelings of members, after they have had to call on the technical services of the funeral director and his staff for a family funeral, should also be explored, but gently. Were needs met? Was the member satisfied? Was the service friendly, understanding, within the cost-ability of the family? This group can keep up a constant self-assessment program. The quality of service should never decline: it should always be improving.

The Money End and Those Earnings

A finance committee can assure the successful and businesslike operation of the organization, auditing in-and-out funds, checking procedures, working closely with the responsible staff to be sure that funds are handled properly. If excess funds accumulate in the checking account, should they be set aside in a savings account? If there is little likelihood that the funds will be needed for some time, should they be invested in stocks and bonds or in a regional or neighboring cooperative organization or in a credit union? A finance committee, whose minds are filled with such practical matters, will find its advice accepted willingly by a board that has entrusted to it the care and oversight of the finances of the organization. Such a committee can arrange for proper outside audits, should that practice be advisable.

After the cooperative pays its bills for supplies, its salaries, sets some money aside for reserves, it confronts the problem of what to do with its excess earning, which private businesses call profit. It doesn't belong to some individual or some distant shareholder in particular but belongs to its owners. The Mesaba Funeral Chapel, in Hibbing, Minnesota, says of its approach, "In addition to savings on the original cost, the Chapel's earnings are distributed in cash and stock certificates at the end of each year to families who have used its services." During the 1967–71 period, the chapel noted that "these cash and stock refunds amounted to some 15 percent of the charge for each funeral. So the total cash and stock refund on a funeral that cost $600 was $90."

The state laws involving incorporation of the cooperative and the distribution of earnings in particular will need to be studied by the organizing board of directors. The system of distributing the excess earnings to the users partly in cash and partly in stock has merit, for it acknowledges not only that the earnings belong to the user but also that the user will wish to share in the further ownership and strengthening of the facility that provided him with such fine service.

Some of the excess earnings belong to those persons and institutions that loaned money to help get things started. Interest, at a reasonable level, is usually expected.

A forward-looking membership will actually want to invest and reinvest as much of its earnings in the cooperative as can possibly be done, while still maintaining that special link with the member-user. It has been suggested by persons evaluating the relatively slow progress of cooperation that its commitment to return profits to its members has held back its development, for funds that in a private-profit business might be used for research and development and other needs are dissipated in small chunks among a large user-constituency in the cooperative.

Consultation with established cooperative leadership will provide useful guidance in this field of profit distribution. Cooperatives need such social capital, but they have to find a mix between capital accumulation and profit redistribution.

Why should "profit" develop in the first place? It is good business sense in a conventional cooperative scheme to charge a little bit more than you need for goods and services, since you have no way of knowing on a day-to-day basis what your financial problems are likely to be. This allows for some flexibility, for some margin of error in business calculations.

An Image Question: Just Another Funeral Parlor?

Image is partly visual, partly psychological. How will the constituency of the Cooperative Funeral Home think of itself? How do the officers and board and committee members and staff and volunteers think of themselves and the Home?

Anyone who does anything "different" has normal fears of being laughed at, scorned, losing the love and time of friends and associates, of being quietly dismissed as a hopeless radical. These are the reasons we usually are reluctant to move ahead or join causes. We are so far along, at this point, in accepting the wisdom, the very inevitability of consumer ownership and control that we know we are going to move ahead. But we want to do it properly. We want to have as members, eventually, everyone who shares our values. No one should turn away for fear of being brushed by some strange foreign taint. How do we proceed?

The answer for most of us is discreet modernity. The Home might appear the same as all the others. It might very well be that Victorian mansion with the cupolas on Main Street. It might be the sleekly effici∠nt-looking modern bank-type building in the Square. It might be the split-level super-bungalow on the corner of Tweedy Estates. Though the Cooperative Funeral Home is an absolutely different kind of institution, it need not cause fear or uncertainty among neighbors and friends by looking "kooky," strange or too wildly different. After all, the organizers themselves are not likely to be "kooky," strange or too wildly different. The Home should reflect the character and stance of its majority.

It is the question of dignity at the time of death that keeps us from thoroughly creative departures in public image. We are controlled, too, by a sense of good business, because we know that, despite the willingness of large numbers of people to invest in and use not-for-private-profit facilities, they are not willing to participate in programs that seem vastly different. Few are ready for that.

The Home should reveal itself, in its outer form, in its literature, in its external appearance as the responsible, dignified program it is. Its image should be positive. The Home's advertisements and literature should not focus exclusively on savings, to avoid seeming to be the "cheap" funeral parlor of the district. The Home should always be described as cooperative—consumer-owned and consumer-controlled. If people don't understand that phraseology immediately (if there is no local tradition of cooperation on which you can call), they will get to understand it as they hear about the benefits of working together. What will convince many people, in the final analysis, will not be your self-jargon but the opportunity to be buried in dignity without great expense, to have survivors handled equitably and responsibly. Not everyone responds to ideology.

The funeral director on your staff should be encouraged to participate in his local funeral trade association. He may encounter some resistance to his participation, because of hostility among private-profit funeral directors to this new counterpoint in what had once been a closed field. The effort, nevertheless, should be made, to make it perfectly clear that the Cooperative Funeral Home is a partner—

albeit consumer in ownership—in the funeral industry. As enough Cooperative Funeral Homes develop throughout the United States, it is possible that a new trade association will develop, one which will serve the intellectual, social and training needs of funeral directors who have aligned themselves with consumer operations.

There should be balance in the views of people. While there needs to be excitement and keen energy expended in the development and maintenance of a cooperative, that institution, that particular mani-festation of cooperation will not save the world. It is part of a far-reaching system of new institutions that, if expanded and relied on and trusted and accepted, may contribute to social transformation.

Advertising

Advertising the services of the Cooperative Funeral Home should be designed not so much to induce people to use its services as to engage people in its purposes: the responsible provision of dignified funeral services on a cooperative basis. This is not as easy as it sounds. Many private funeral houses that advertise their existence emphasize their "service," their "dignity." These funeral supermarkets do their funeral equivalent of A & P's "We Care" slogan and consumers are too often impressed. The unsmiling but concerned look of the funeral director, whose photograph sometimes appears on those ads, gives an image of businesslike responsibility which often changes when you are in the door. You have been caught.

Because of the uniqueness of the cooperative approach, it is likely that word-of-mouth advertising will be the most important. That approach connects friends with friends, whose good words about the fine program and selfless approach of the cooperative draw in new supporters, not mere users. When the facility is new, perhaps newspaper stories and articles will appear based on its special character. But after a while the story will no longer be new and the Home's staff, board, committee people and members will have to wrestle with the problem of support.

Telling others about the cooperative, which is what advertising is all about, provides those directing the promotional and educational effort with a stimulating task.

A basically different attitude may need to be explored, because of the need for support-efforts. The work of promotion is not the work of one committee; suppose it should fail? Thus, the idea of promoting the cooperative should be seen and understood as everyone's job. The job of the promotional and educational people must be to provide the tools and the insight which will help every concerned member. Another way of looking at this is to view the job of special committees working on advertising as the creation of an atmosphere of cooperative funeral activity.

That is what good advertising does. The advertised "product" becomes a part of the atmosphere. Mention soup, for example, and the mind usually conjures up "Campbell's." The cooperative can create such an atmosphere and know that it is for a purpose beyond mere sales and profits. "People helping themselves and each other in one of life's basic tasks" is a proud image and worth casting on the waters. That people will benefit financially will sustain the wisdom of the approach: it *pays* to cooperate.

The most effective advertising, no matter who is doing it, reminds people—here, there, everywhere—that the product or service exists. Obviously, a funeral home is not soup. It's not underarm deodorant. But it is an essential service and can be as familiar as the emergency police phone number is to residents of New York City, which, though rarely used by the average person, is available and *known*. A persistent educational and promotional program is required which, with the aid and experience and focus of a committee working on the subject, becomes the concern of every person involved and drawn to the idea of consumer cooperation.

The community's size and advertising opportunities will vary. Some approaches may be unworkable (though it is good to try them before you pronounce them dead), others will catch on.

There is, of course, paid advertising. A little box in the obituary section, where the private houses sell their wares, can work for you. Including the line CONSUMER-OWNED AND CONSUMER-CONTROLLED will catch the attention of those seeking your services. A line drawing attention to your encouragement of advance planning may be helpful, too. The ad should be more than the announcement of the name of your organization. Your name alone is not that splendid—even with the word "cooperative" in it. Something more is needed: it's that extra line, the words that make you clearly different, that will attract. Using the obituary page, of course, makes your announcement available to the casual readers of obituaries as well as to those looking for quick assistance. (If your Home is available to the person who can become a member on the spot, there is no reason you should not advertise with that spirit in mind. Such memberships build lasting friendships: your service has been provided, you will be available again the next time.)

The question of advertising your prices is an interesting one. The funeral industry is supervised by regulatory agencies, usually manned by funeral directors. That's the story of regulatory agencies in American society . . . the supervised are the supervisors! Consumer dominance of regulatory agencies, a logical development if consumers are to have control over services they alone use, is still in the future. Trade groups, like funeral directors, pharmacists and others set up and maintain their own codes of what is ethical, a practice which, while peculiar, does govern the behavior of their members.

Sometimes the codes change, but they may require legal action by concerned people to break through. If the funeral trade in your state does not "permit" advertising of prices, since it has deemed it "unethical," it should probably be challenged. Such restriction eliminates competition among funeral directors; it removes from the consumer his natural right to do comparison shopping, which, if he could exercise it, would keep him from becoming a prisoner of the trade. Licensed funeral directors will know the price-advertising situation in your state, as will the regulatory agency.

Advertising prices may be considered by some people to be tasteless. Advanced consumers need to break out of the silly sentiment which requires a no-see, no-talk, no-hear monkey policy on questions of cost. An advanced consumer recognizes that the unwillingness to discuss prices at the time of death, or preferably before, is precisely the reason that funeral directors have been able to build such high price structures. Funeral directors in the private-profit spirit too often embarrass untrained consumers, who might wince at high prices and ask if less money could be spent, by suggesting low prices mean "cheap." And because we have these strange ideas that, in respect for the dead, "It's not nice to talk prices," we're down the slippery path.

The basic literature of the Home will have many advertising uses. We often see that friendly folders of community-service organizations have a home on church literature tables, are posted on the bulletin boards of a hundred organizations, since they are not commercial sales messages. Such items are a useful part of an advertising program. They attract new people and also build a sense of pride in existing members, essential for that sense of presence we want to build for our cooperative.

There is no reason why an ongoing cooperative could not send out calendars to its members, to supportive religious groups. Posters in local cooperative shops make just as much sense for you as they do for the local concert group.

There are many organizations sympathetic to your purposes that send out regular newsletters to their members. Sometimes they will permit you to tell your story in them, or, if their material is sent out in an envelope, permit you to enclose your folder. The latter is ideal, for your material will have and should have an easy-to-clip-out coupon for those people who want more information.

The local radio station will permit public-service advertising and is in fact required to offer some. There is the likelihood that your activity may not be considered public service by the station, but it is worth asking about. Getting acquainted with the station's program director may open up a series of interviews about your program and concern, which might be more useful in the long run. Local television offers the same opportunities. You *are* news and you *are* service.

The basic point is that advertising need not be expensive. There are many ways to tell your story. Spend money if you have to, but it is good business and good psychology to tell your community-service story in the least costly way possible. Essentially, in spirit, there is no difference between your service business and the work of the Red Cross and the Heart Fund, though you will get arguments from some people on that point. We need to stretch our minds, that's all. If we have something that is *good* for the community, we should do everything in our power and energy to reach it.

Printing and Literature Needs

Let us look at the printing and literature needs of a Cooperative Funeral Home. All of the Home's literature is designed to stimulate thinking about funeral practices, to encourage people to plan ahead, to enable people to make plans and to tell the story of the Home to inquiring visitors.

There are some items without which no organization can function. First is that basic folder, which tells the story and invites inquiry. This can be a simple 8½″ × 11″ sheet, with writing and art work on both sides, folded to fit into a #10 business envelope. This is also the right size for most literature racks and it fits well on a literature table, since it is the size of most promotional material likely to be found there. Analyze the junk mail you receive from organizations desiring your support. Usually an attractive folder will suggest designs and type approaches that can be used to good effect by you.

The usual letterhead and envelopes, with the name and address of the cooperative clearly marked, with type big enough for an older person or a person with poor sight to read without the aid of glasses, are essential. It is not immodest to use large type. It is intelligent if your purpose is communication. Groups sometimes are willing to make their names stand out in bold type, but then the addresses and phone numbers are so small they cannot be read easily. Begin boldly, and continue that way.

The funeral director needs calling cards. And so do those board members who have the job of getting the message out. They can be given to people who want to follow up a conversation with you; they can be sent to a friend you'd like to engage in the work, along with a piece of literature. There are a hundred uses.

There is need for a poster. A small one on 8½″ × 11″ stock is the most adaptable. Large posters take room and tend to be removed from bulletin boards by people who want the space. Some groups have used 5″ × 7″ or even 3″ × 5″ cards to good avail. The smaller the poster, the longer it stays up: strange but true! The standard poster, telling about the Home, describing its program briefly, printed in an attractive color, will tell your story in your absence. It is a continuing message, a reminder, a conversation starter, a signal to your own members that you are alive and active.

Too often we think of literature, posters and other media only in terms of new people. They keep us in touch with existing members as well. When your own members begin to forget about you, you are in trouble.

The local printer will help the Home find the best and most inexpensive approach to printing. Visit two or three. It is probably a good idea, if you have only so-called "job shops" in your area, to have an idea of what you want, with even some thought about the kinds of type (look at your newspaper and clip out samples of what you have in mind), since many job shops have no artistic experience but can do excellent printing jobs. An artist in the Home group will have some insight into design, type faces and perhaps even printing knowledge and experience.

The Home will need special materials to help people plan ahead. Study planning materials issued by memorial societies and print a supply of your own.

Beyond these essentials, there are other things that can be done. Books in the field can be made available in the office of the Home. Magazines of the trade can be displayed, since Home people will want to be familiar with the industry's work. Copies of Morgan's *Manual* can be offered for sale. We need to educate, for education is part of our reason for being!

Atmosphere Questions

What should the atmosphere of a Cooperative Funeral Home be like?

What is atmosphere?

Consider the immediate impression of the typical funeral home. Subdued light, hush-hush quiet, thick rugs, dark drapes greet the visitor. That is the environment that reaches you when you enter for a funeral occasion or to do business.

But the environment of our cooperative is more than an environment of death. It is also a place for meetings. It is a place where people can come to plan their own funerals in advance. What, then, must we do?

Two entrances are possible, one for funeral occasions, the other for business and meetings. The business entrance can lead into conference rooms, into living rooms, into offices. An attractive, comfortable sense of purpose should be communicated. Efficiency and organization should be apparent. A teaching/learning spirit should be communicated. What are the examples we might refer to? The busy office of the high school principal is one: he has his place for privacy, yet teachers come in and out, do their business, reach for their mail. Students rush in and rush out, too. There are chairs for people waiting to see school officials. There are signs and posters on the wall. The phone rings and is answered. There is literature on a rack or table. There is a vibrancy communicated in a school office: it's a busy place. We have reason to believe we will be busy, too: we should be prepared for it.

Our activity need not interfere with the funeral occasion. That's the best argument for separate entrances. On the other hand, the facility available may not permit a choice. A division of the day might then be necessary, restricting the busy in-and-out robustness of an organization at work to hours of the day not likely to be needed for funerals and funeral occasions. Those persons using the facilities for funerals deserve privacy (they are, after all, the reason the Home was organized) and should be protected.

The tastes of the organizing group set the stage for all those who follow. There is no wisdom in being so conventional or so avant-garde that every time a new board is elected there needs to be a big discussion about the atmosphere and costs incurred to meet the new needs. There is something to be said for getting the reaction of many members to their first facility: it is *their* cooperative. Practical answers are necessary, since unlimited funds are not likely to be available; responding in some way to the needs and desires of the pioneers joining in with you should nevertheless be acknowledged.

Expect differences of opinion when decisions are being made—and have to be made—about the atmosphere. Under such circumstances, compromises are necessary. No one should be offended. Consequently, the path likely to be chosen will be more or less conservative. That is the way with the world. Actual use of the facility, actual experience with the many problems and choices facing a community-service organization will inform the paid and volunteer staff alike, and the board will need to be prepared to respond to proposals for change, improvement, remodeling, expansion and the like. If people are excited about their own cooperative, they will have suggestions for improvement. As difficult as it is, leadership groups have to learn to say No. They also have to learn to listen and take all suggestions seriously. The cooperative needs the continuing support of those whose ideas are turned down, too.

A philosophy of management is involved here, which is well worth considering. Too many organizations stifle dissent, rather than hear it and absorb it; too many crudely set aside suggestions from well-meaning and experienced people; too many just listen to the "important" people in their organization. In a cooperative, everyone is important. That delicate balance between the ideal and the real, the practical and the idealistic, must be maintained in a spirit of friendly and open sharing. Sometimes organizational leadership, having worked hard to build something for its group, develops a vested interest in "what is" and fails to respond courteously to suggestions for change. It is understandable, but the winds of cooperative development and growth and the engagement of persons also bring in proposals of change which must sometimes be implemented. Democracy, in a spirit of consensus rather than of contentiousness, is beautiful. For one side or the other to "win" in some dispute is too often to lose the losers. In a cooperative, where we should all be the gainers, we need to learn and practice the fine, winning arts of friendly persuasion, the politics of fun, the gentleness of the lamb with a lion's purpose. Tough, but worth it: the process is the secret entrance to a successful co-op.

How Do We Contribute to Others?

We can serve nonmember needs. An effective Cooperative Funeral Home sends out ripples into the community. Just its existence provides a counterpoint to the familiar focus: it seems the same, yet it is different.

For one thing, the existence of a cooperative will stimulate competition in the funeral field. It's a new entry in the race. The effect of competition may very well be to lower rates in the private-profit establishment long, too long, unchallenged. Thus the cooperative will help the entire community, those unwilling to join and even those who might be philosophically hostile to its purposes. In most communities where cooperatives are formed and stand up high enough to attract attention, private-profit organizations take notice and respond in the best way they know: lowering the prices. Since they must maintain profit for the sake of their owners, they are not likely to come close to the price at which a cooperative can afford to function. If the private-profit directors collaborate in a deliberate low-price uniform strategy to put the cooperative out of business, they are probably violating the law. Thus, in a general private-enterprise environment, the cooperative can play a useful, corrective role on behalf of all consumers.

The cooperative which goes beyond merely disposing of bodies to the conduct of educational activities will help people think about death. Everyone who responds and participates will gain, not necessarily members. Even the announcement of open, public meetings will have effect on people who wouldn't be caught dead attending a cooperative meeting of any kind. Residents in the community should be asked to think about their deaths and consequently their lives. The net effect of such programming, in a broad and real sense, should be a heightening of the quality of life in most communities, for people who can think about death and become prepared for it are likely to put more energy into their lives, use the time they have more wisely and happily, refocus their daily orientations.

Every piece of literature that reaches into a home—calling perhaps for planning or for membership in the cooperative—will produce change. Families might resist or even reject the invitation. But the challenge remains: a new consciousness, a new life, a new willingness to face up to death questions. And it can happen. Thousands and thousands of pieces of literature distributed by memorial societies, inviting membership, while perhaps unanswered in terms of society membership, are answered through new thinking.

When the cooperative offers a speaker to a school and the invitation is accepted, the ramifications are tremendous. Each student returns home and discussions ensue. There is a quick reaction, in families where superstition or stress dominate, which might ask if the schools are losing their heads and dabbling in the undabblable, but most families on reflection will be surprised and appreciative. As in sex education, the schools may wind up doing what parents are unwilling to do. The funeral directors also realize the importance of schools, for many of the trade associations have offered speakers to schools as part of their counteroffensive to the new consumer movement.

What happens to a discussion heard on the radio or viewed on television? It is heard. It is remembered. Think of the video impressions in your mind. Programs of a dozen years ago remain, short flashbacks. On a subject that reaches close to the heart, the memory pattern is stronger. It is in the cooperative's interest to seek such opportunities. It will help the cooperative in its immediate aims and contribute to new thinking in the general community as well.

There is another need in American society which will be met in part by the appearance of a Cooperative Funeral Home. Americans, though famed for their committee-itis, their voluntarist impulse, their eagerness to do good, have by and large left worthwhile efforts to a fairly small group. They are somewhat cynical about the business of helping others, fearing that in even clearly generous activities someone is gaining something from it. Or they mutter, perhaps enviously, about the glory and the power and the attention given to such volunteers.

When it comes to practical questions, to alternative institutions, to getting City Hall to do something, many Americans fall back on the apathy line: too many of the others (not they themselves, of course) are apathetic. Even if large numbers of persons were persuaded to engage in the pursuit of reform, nothing would happen, they say. There is too much power in the hands of big business, they say (of course, they're right), and public officials do not want to enter into combat with local power business and social and class elites, they say (of course, they're right), so the little people, ordinary consumers, can't expect anything to happen (of course, they're wrong).

When small groups of people, like those organizing a Cooperative Funeral Home, break through the apathy gap, gather supporters, borrow money, construct a building, perform valuable services, they produce change. And they contribute through their practical acts to a revitalization of the idea that people do and can make a difference. The revival of that activist instinct is profoundly needed in American society, increasingly dependent on someone up there, out there, to do something. The world needs restoration, that's clear, and the people in it need to have restored to them their sense of power. Dictatorships flourish when people give up and let "others" do the business of living for them, the business of making decisions. Big brothers are, unfortunately, always available for a society of people who prefer leadership to personal action. Through cooperatives, in the funeral field as elsewhere, Americans keep alive the significance of the person, of the one, of self-help. And they nourish the notion that those selves, in a spirit of mutual aid, do not—in their common program—need to diminish the significance of any single self. Every person, every *one,* when cooperation flourishes, remains important. Equality lives in cooperation; it does not live in dependence.

One Cooperative Funeral Home in Tuscaloosa or Portland or New York, we should emphasize again, is not going to change the world. But the people active in the Home are not going to let the world change them. Through little activities in the little and big towns of America, new sentiments are born. The concept of a "free people" did not emerge from the head of one man, or even from the heads of several. Its deep roots in economic development, in religious thinking, in the struggles of people wishing the end of financial, royal or political tyrannies over the centuries have been thoroughly analyzed. We know for sure, regardless of its origins, that the concept is here, that it is evident. But ideas slip away, too, when people permit themselves to be discouraged.

There are forces and institutions and leaders who would seem to deny the right of people to fulfill themselves as economic and social persons. Those people who would be free need to practice their freedom, lest its practice be forgotten, its liberating spirit only a vaguely remembered act of forefathers in distant history. If Tuscaloosans and Portlanders and New Yorkers accept the nay-saying and "ethical codes" and rules and regulations and bad-mouthing of those who do not want these new cooperatives to form, the price we shall have to pay in the long run will be the destruction of the ideas we cherish. In saying that we give up, in accepting the No of people who do not want us to trouble the waters of the economic system, we become ourselves another drop in the apathetic seas, contemptible for having once believed, scorning ourselves too for having become faithless. The price for betrayal is high; the reward for trying is a good life spent in the pursuit of an even better life for oneself and others.

Now a Cooperative Funeral Home is clear in your mind, you and your friends have become convinced, have moved ahead. Decisions have been made.

It's time for the announcement of Opening Day. How will the community receive the reality?

Opening Day

8

Here we are. Six months or a year or two of planning and hard work are over. The doors of the Cooperative Funeral Home are ready to open.

Are we ready?

We are, if we have laid the proper base.

Many small businesses fail, often because an inadequate study of the market potential has been made and usually because the investors truly believe that their product and service are so good that people will flock to their business once an announcement has been posted, an ad placed in the local newspaper and the doors open. Unfortunately, that approach will not work in the cooperative setting either.

In the period of organization, the cooperative will have built its business, that is to say, its constituency, carefully and systematically. Once the doors are opened, it is too late to look for members. It must be done ahead of time. There will be an air of expectation about the new co-op. Everyone will know that it has been in the planning stage. Everyone will have participated in discussions. Everyone will have seen announcements on bulletin boards and heard references in meetings in all kinds of groups.

The air of expectation cannot be puffed into the establishment at the last moment. The opening of the doors is the culmination of an arduous period of enterprise, not the beginning. That is an important point for organizers of a community service to recognize.

The community should have shared in the development all along the way, hearing progress reports, seeing literature, being drawn into membership. The nonparticipating general community should have a good idea of what's happening. The Cooperative Funeral Home should not be a secret, an unexploded missile to surprise everyone on Opening Day.

Careful Preparation Needed

A realistic Opening Day should be announced months in advance. There are so many things that can go wrong in planning that it is well to acknowledge the possibility of delays. Equipment doesn't arrive, the right staff can't be found, the literature isn't produced and circulated in time. We are used to such delays in Grand Openings, but we should do our best to achieve our aim. Allowing enough time should do it.

An Opening Day can be mere coffee and cake, but it can also be a variety of events. If a candy store were our aim, coffee and cake and candy might be enough, but we are talking about a major, multidimensional facility, with many strands of input and concern from the overall community. Death and our Home tap into the very psyche of the community. Not only are our members naturally interested in the project, there are others who have a stake in its dignified success. (Some will have bet on its failure, too.)

Curiosity is for many people the prime motive behind attendance at an Opening Day. For people involved in the work and planning, the end of a period of labor is being celebrated. But for those on the fringes, the event is one of "Let's go see." Cynics in the wings, who might even have become members, now have to swallow their words: they decided to wait and see, now they can see.

What are the possibilities for Opening Day activities? One or all of the following are workable (you might need an Opening Week to handle them all):

1. An all-day Open House, inviting members and their friends to visit the facility. A special time for these people honors the faith they had in the enterprise. In that connection, food and drink can be

served, especially during the lunch period. Saturday and Sunday are natural days for the occasion, since more people are likely to be available both to do the work and to come sometime during the day.

An all-day Open House can be a time when the various activities of the cooperative can be fully explained to visitors. One of the conference rooms can be the center for the social-service group, who, through signs and mimeographed literature and their personal stories, can describe the programs they plan to pursue. Every visitor to that room is a potential member of that committee. And so on with other committees.

Open House is a constant tour of the facilities. Signs should be up on every door and every closet explaining the contents. Members should feel free to visit the casket-storage room, the cellar, the attic. The operating-room aspect of preparation rooms—with their clinical feeling, their strange tools—may not be attractive to many visitors, but everyone should be allowed and encouraged to see everything. This will certainly be the first time most of them have ever been invited to inspect such a room! There should be no mysteries perpetuated by a Cooperative Funeral Home. The more the visitor sees, the more the facility is his. It's that simple. Committee members with general understanding can lead groups, or individuals can be free to wander. At any rate, Opening Day will make it clear: there are no secrets in the cooperative.

2. An all-day Open House, inviting the *entire community* as well as members and their friends to visit the facility. This is much more work, but the effort may be well spent, since many persons coming that day may be giving thought, are likely to be giving thought, to membership. A membership table, front and center in the lobby, is a strong emphasis in this kind of Open House.

If concern about security of property exists, the Open House can be more structured. A visitor can be given a map to the Home, which will guide him through a clearly marked path (even rope guides can be used) that will take him to the various corners of the house and then leave him in the room where the refreshments are available. Board and committee members, placed along the route, can offer explanations to their visitors, responding to questions, describing various committee functions and Home activities and so on.

3. Complementing a part-day or all-day Open House can be a series of special educational gatherings. A larger room in the Home can be used for a continuing seminar, or a special half-hour or one-hour-long meeting, to which each visitor will be invited.

This meeting can be the first gathering point for visitors as they enter. When the room is full, a board member may use the opportunity to tell the visitors exactly what the Home is all about, explain its many services, discuss its approach to service and costs and *then* invite people to take the tour.

4. Specialized occasions can be held during Open House day, too, either in the Home or in adjacent facilities for special-interest groups such as members of the clergy. In these cases the probing will be deeper, the explanations more thorough and far-reaching. Special invitations can be issued for these seminars, which might include a social aspect as well. It could be an event arranged in cooperation with the local council of churches or ministerial association.

Other special-interest groups might include the teaching profession, those who serve all ages up through college. If there is reason to believe that large numbers of professionals may attend, a division of that group may be invited. Many high school teachers, for example, may welcome a chance to discuss death education during Open House day.

Psychologists on school staffs and in private practice may wish a special time, too.

How does one know who might be interested? The experience of the Home's key people has the answer. Teachers associated with the Home will know what is happening among their colleagues. Psychologically trained people will know their associates' orientations and reactions. Members of the clergy will know the needs of their group, too. It is possible that a special reception for such groups may be held, using it as a recruiting basis for future seminars and occasions.

Specialized groups value panels of speakers, whose views on the subject may be varied and provocative. A distinguished visitor from a distance can be attractive, too, providing insight in an area of expertise: a leader in the field of death education, a psychologist with new insights into the counseling of survivors, a minister with a special point of view about the responsibility of the religious community, a philosopher/writer on new perspectives for those who know they are about to die. These events can be a part of the fabric of pre-Opening Day development as well.

5. There is nothing wrong with building Opening Day events around a famous personality. There may be, in *your* constituency, some person of distinction and fame who would not mind being the "calling card" for an important event. A theater figure, a writer, a political figure will understand how these things work: these people are familiar with the technique and may not mind making themselves available for your (and hopefully, their) purpose. A local and popular disc jockey, a radio and television personality can be an attraction. These people are accustomed to audiences and people who want autographs. If we are reluctant to tap into that strange characteristic of people which draws us to the rich and the famous, we can avoid it, but before discarding it the organizers should think through thoroughly the original purpose of Open House, which is to get visitors. What will work in your community? That is the question.

The curiosity of visitors extends to the costs of a funeral. Unless the Home's Opening Day organizers speak to this question, it will continue to lurk in the minds of visitors. Therefore, arrangements should be made for a poster or a piece of literature which spells out clearly the not-for-private-profit character of the Home. A special table, booth or wall can make absolutely clear the charges of the Home for particular services. While people will be impressed with the openness of the Home, they will be overwhelmed by an openness about the price structure, both of which are actually beyond the ordinary experience of most people. The deliberate destruction of secrets is a conscious policy and program of cooperatives, and the price conspiracy of the private-profit industry can be ended with one clear program: let everybody know everything. It should be made equally clear that any excess earnings beyond costs of operating the facility and needed reserves will return to member-users. Several funeral plans can be outlined in detail, so that there will be no doubt that this is (at last) one facility in which the consumer has choice.

Why not be bold? A piece of literature or poster can ask the question, "Planning to spend $1000?" Subtitles can say, "A basic funeral . . . see plan #2 . . . will cost $600. That leaves $400 for the Heart

Fund, for a donation to the library in the name of the deceased, for the local hospital, for the education of the children." Let us tap into consumer wisdom. Everyone knows a bargain. Everyone has a favored cause. Through such simple acts of comparison we contribute to a reversing of funeral psychology and show the truer wisdom of less expense. Dollars are dollars. The Home does not hesitate to discuss alternative uses of the body, and is helpful to its members wishing the other-than-ordinary kind of funeral approach; there is no reason why the Home cannot discuss alternative uses of funds that might otherwise be spent on a funeral. Lavishing money on the dead, we would be saying, does not honor the dead or ennoble the living. We *can* honor the dead and ennoble the living by letting the money continue to work, in the name of the deceased, among the survivors.

It is conceivable that a Cooperative Funeral Home, building this emphasis with the consent of its members, may itself wish to have a Cooperative Foundation through which funds that otherwise might be used on funerals could be directed to worthwhile community functions. It is a challenging idea. For that matter, by the time the organizers have reached Opening Day, their bodies may be tired but their minds will be filled with many new ideas bursting to see the light of day. That's what happens in cooperation: people are liberated and want to do more. Imagination is fostered when people are free of their old chains. Creativity is unleashed.

We are open for business. Except for the public educational activity and the pricing structure and the Opening Day events, wrapped up in the specialness of Consumer Cooperation, we are a discreetly ordinary Cooperative Funeral Home. The day-by-day service of the Home begins. The mind stretches to new possibilities. Have we merely touched the tip of the service iceberg?

An examination of variants and extensions of what we have created is in order.

Some Variants
for a Future Time

9

"DANCE ON SATURDAY NIGHT at the Cooperative Funeral Home in memory of Bill Jervis."

"SAUERBRATEN DINNER, honoring the memory of our friend William Kinkel, to be held Tuesday at 7:00 P.M. at the Cooperative Funeral Home. Please come. Send your reservations to . . ."

"POETRY READING in the Fireplace Room at the Cooperative Funeral Home on Thursday at 8:00 P.M. to recall the life and concerns of Melissa Blankton."

Strange announcements? Maybe to our untrained eyes. We are not used to associating these events with a funeral home.

But all things are possible. Simple self-determination, the taproot of our activity, says they are.

New Times Suggest New Approaches

The austere modernity of our Cooperative Funeral Home, the sensible and businesslike provision of services to members, the related educational programs, the sense of community service, the overcoming of old prejudices and fears, the courageous development of a cooperative counterpoint in the funeral field have filled us with an understandable self-admiration. We like ourselves for what we have done. We like the Home. We like its members. We are suitably impressed.

It will have been said that the idea of our rather conventional and only slightly different Cooperative Funeral Home should be enough. Let us rest on our laurels. There it is, our Home, let us now sit back. The curious act of creation, we need to recall, leads to parenthood and perhaps, if we liked the experience, to more acts of creation. Ideas produce ideas. The vigorous pursuit of new services, like the pursuit of truths, opens up new vistas, new possibilities in the field.

That is what will happen to everyone who has contributed to the development of a Cooperative Funeral Home. More will be needed. The energized membership will ask for more from the board. The board will debate the readiness of members to accept new ideas. The back and forth of excited personalities will produce volcanoes of proposals, whose fine ash will touch all.

Moderate conventionality will satisfy most people. Others want to move on. This chapter is for those adventurers. If a hundred or a thousand Cooperative Funeral Homes stop at Chapter 8, there is no cause to complain: a world will have changed. But there are new worlds.

Some people will want to move far beyond the discreet suggestions made so far: the establishment of a memorial society, the development of a Cooperative Funeral Home. They will want to incorporate ideas that are closer to what they conceive to be the "future" of death. They should not be discouraged. I will not discourage them. If a group of pioneers senses its constituency to be ready for further explorations, they should by all and any means take the leap.

Of course, the key is in understanding the constituency. New York City, large, cumbersome, with a thousand communities within it, probably has many groups ready for further development in funeral reform. The same might be said of Chicago, Los Angeles, San Francisco and dozens of other large cities. Bits and pieces of total reform might be used in smaller communities, where the market for advanced services might be smaller but nevertheless ready for diverse and surprisingly different approaches.

The costs of unusual programming will not be calculated here. Each has its range of possibilities, within small and larger budgets.

If a Cooperative Funeral Home takes the position that it wishes to provide a freedom of choice for consumers, then it must allow its facilities to provide the range of responses of which we humans are capable.

So depressed are many Americans by their experience with the typical funeral home, they may find it difficult to deal with other concepts. Yet a truly service-oriented Cooperative Funeral Home, it can be argued, needs to be open to the broadest possibilities.

Why should we conform at the time of death? Many people, trying to be as true to themselves as possible for a lifetime, don't want to go the way everyone else does. Their very last act should be true to their lives, they might well say; the funeral should not be a defeat but a last victory over the conforming forces of society, those forces that say there is only one way to do things, one way to live, one way to die. Break out. Live. Let the world know you are truly alive. We can hear those persons now! Sing out loud in public places: praise be to the souls who dare to be different!

Let us pursue some of the possibilities.

Rooms for Memorial Meetings

It will be difficult for the typical Cooperative Funeral Home to switch rooms back and forth from the funereal to the festive (yes, festive), wheeling out the casket after one kind of occasion and changing the drapes to suit the moods of those who might prefer a more vigorous and lighthearted kind of occasion. All-purpose rooms will take lots of work and lots of planning. It might be better, if facilities permit, to have different kinds of rooms for different kinds of purposes.

In our earlier discussion about memorial meetings, it became clear that variety is desirable. Thus a memorial meeting may require just a large plain room with lots of comfortable seats. A fireplace at one end is ideal, for fire is one of the universal symbols of warmth, of the mix of new life and old life accepted and cherished by many. As the fire dies down, the last speakers having shared their recollections, the attenders sit in silence as the fire draws its last strength from the wood that gave it life. The family rises, the signal for the group to shake hands, everyone strengthened by a beautiful experience of sharing.

Refreshments may be served now at one end of the room or in an adjoining room. The life, not the body and death, of the deceased friend, is with the group, as friends greet each other, receive the introductions of new people, and talk about the sights and sounds and recollections of the life they have been reviewing.

After food has been served and visitors have departed, the immediate survivors leave for the living of a different life. While the refreshment crew cleans up, the attendants of the Cooperative Funeral Home begin the process of setting the chairs in the main Fireplace Room for another meeting scheduled to begin soon.

An aficionado of folk dancing has died the week before, and his relatives and friends, faithful to his wishes, have arranged a folk dance at the Home for those who had shared in that interest. The chairs are placed along the walls, the rug is rolled up, the fire is relighted, and the record-playing system rolled into the room. Earlier, favorite dance records of the deceased person had been picked up by someone from the Home. A fresh urn of coffee is being made and a supply of apples and oranges laid out. That is the style of the folk-dance society; that will be today's style. Three hours have been reserved for the dance.

The folk-dance leader arrives a few minutes before the appointed time to check on arrangements. Then the guests begin to arrive. When a sizable group is assembled, the leader stands on a chair and says, slowly and clearly, "Our friend, Bill Jamison, loved to dance. Dancing was, in fact, his life. A student of folk dancing, a great teacher, he saw the world through the dancing feet of people who had set aside their worries and grievances to spend time following the patterns and paces of the folk art. Bill asked us to remember him with a last dance, here at the Home. He asked that we laugh and eat and dance, in the way we did when he was with us. This is the way he wants to be remembered. Turn up the music. Let's dance, to the memory of Bill Jamison!"

For almost three hours, the familiar music heightened the sense of Bill's presence. He was there dancing. One expected him to stand up and announce the next dance, the way he often did at the usual meetings of the group. The dance over, the exhausted friends left with a warm glow. Bill would not be forgotten.

While the dancers were in their third hour, a kitchen crew was working on the last preparations for a dinner scheduled in the Fireplace Room for six that evening. The dinner was to recall the life and memory of a man, Arthur Houser, who for years had taught math in the local high school but who nourished a private life as a splendid cook. His favorite, as his friends well knew from events he had hosted at the fraternal hall, was sauerbraten. On his planning forms, Arthur had said he did not want to have people look at his body or at his casket; he wanted, instead, a dinner in the Fireplace Room of the Home for his friends. The menu was to be sauerbraten. He asked that his favorite "oom-pah" music be played over the room's loudspeakers and that German beer be served with the meal. He made it clear in his "Expression of Wishes" that he didn't want a lot of sad speeches during the meal. Between the meal and dessert, he said, he would like the high school principal, a good friend of his, to read a poem of which Arthur was particularly fond. That was all. The music turned on again, the eating and drinking continued. Every bite eaten, every drop of beer swigged became a reminder of Arthur's presence on earth among his friends.

It is nine o'clock now at the Home. The dinner group has left. The tables are being folded and the chairs stacked. The clatter of the last dishes being washed can be heard in the now quiet cooperative.

At 9:30, a small group is due to arrive. They want the fire burning and a circle of soft-cushioned chairs around the fireplace. Mostly elderly people, the group wants a silent meeting of recollection for ancient Aunt Jane, who had lived at the nearby Senior Citizens' Center. When she died, her body had been cremated, as she suggested. The handful of people who lived with her at the Center had been asked to come together a week later, to sit around the fireplace and to speak if they wished about her life.

The fireplace roaring at first, quieting into a steady rhythm of wind and puff and crackle, hosts the two dozen friends of Aunt Jane's. No one says anything at first. Then one person speaks of the first time, some ten years earlier, that she met Aunt Jane, the day she came to the Center to live. Aunt Jane was spunky then, a little irritated that she had to move in with what she called "crotchety old people." She found, instead, people like herself, full of games, good conversation, enjoyment of flowers. The years passed. The friend recalls speaking to Aunt Jane just a couple of weeks ago about her grand entrance ten years before. "Aunt Jane looked up at me," the speaker quietly says, "and told me that she wished everyone of every age could have the good life she had had these past ten years. People *need* friends." Smiles of recognition pass around the gathered group. Another speaks of her "green thumb" with flowers, another of her unheralded work of comforting one or another of them who had a sudden feeling of loneliness and isolation, another reads a poem which reminds the speaker of Aunt Jane, another remembers the time Aunt Jane decorated the lobby of the Center for the expected arrival of relatives from Des Moines and how happy she was about the visit. An hour passes. There are gaps of peaceful silence between the messages. Betty Jo, as the reserved time draws to a close, says, "We will always remember Aunt Jane. Thank God for everything she has done for us." The group stands up slowly, puts on coats and walks out together, returning to the Center, their mutual home until death.

So much for the Fireplace Room. Its capacity to contain the souls of the living and the dead is clear, its infinite flexibility revealed through its actual uses. What the Spirit declared should be, can be.

The Cheerful Rooms

There is another workable dimension in an avant-garde facility, that is, one big enough to include a variety of rooms for other purposes. Why not cheerful rooms, decorated with bright yellow flowers and red stripes? Why not a bright blue room, a red room? These can be the focus for occasions with body display or with closed caskets as well. People might wish to pursue the conventional (perhaps for the sake of the family, a gentle recognition of debt to others), but to do it in an unconventional setting.

There may be a woman, the party-giver of the community, who will want bright streamers around her closed coffin and sent from corner to corner of the gaily decorated room. People thinking of her thought of parties. She had requested in her funeral planning forms that her Lutheran minister conduct a religious service for her, that the Flower and Stripes Room be used, that her friends be given, on entering the room, a specially printed copy of a poem she had written about the joys and gift of friends and life. Her minister has a copy of her

"Expression of Wishes"; he knows her special spirit and, while he is accustomed to thinking about funereal occasions in more somber settings, he knows that he had a character in Millicent Dunkin; he does a good job. Somehow the atmosphere, brimful of life and cheer and color (and potted live flowers around the room, her special request) makes his otherwise usually somber message about ashes to ashes and dust to dust seem almost a cheerful message. The gathering senses it; the weeping relatives sense it; the organist (a volunteer working with the Home) senses it. "This is the way Millie wanted it," friends said to each other, shaking hands after the service. They line up to shake the hands of the relatives and then proceed to the fleet of cars outside. Their destination is the Livingston Cemetery, some miles away, where the body, with the usual ceremony, will be placed in the Dunkin family plot.

People's lives are reflected in these occasions of death. Current practice takes bodies into environments unseemly for most people. The revolution of values occasioned by the new consumerism asks that the last public occasion be like life. Or be what was wanted. The purpose of the Home is to do the best it can to provide the occasion requested by the deceased, responding in good spirit to these last wishes. The Home, given its commitment to freedom of choice, could not criticize. It is not in a position to criticize. It exists to serve.

The typical funeral home is organized to repress the individual and his requests. Only one atmosphere is permitted: somber, sobersides, straight. While the cooperative can provide that response if the consumer wishes it, there is no doubt but that the new availability of choice to consumers will prompt an easier and lighter flow of funeral events. Infinite varieties will appear. Mark death we must, but in our Home we shall have a role in determining how it shall be marked.

Part of the magic of the Cooperative Funeral Home is that it provides a place where volunteer friends of the deceased can do their supportive work: the meal, the party, the flowers. The less dependence on staff, the less costly the occasion. No private-profit funeral parlor permits the engagement of friends and relatives in the conduct of funeral occasions. Liberated consumers, operating in their own Home, have restored to them their fundamental right to create a last special time of recollection of their friend.

One room can be devoted to music.

Another can be a Little Theater, where slides and films about the life of the deceased friend can be shown. Artistic performances can be viewed. "This Is Your Life" performances, offered by friends, can heighten the life of the dead by recalling in dramatic form events of times gone by.

Poetry readings, performances of Shakespeare, a violinist's rendition of loved music can take place if the Home has arranged facilities for them.

An adaptable facility, representing adaptable people, will be open to consumer choice. Splendid and healthy, it will replace the arthritic knee-bending sorrow of current practice. The mystery of funeral practice will disappear as consumers take over the practices related to death, conduct the occasions of sorrow and celebration. Death belongs to consumers. It is, after all, they who die. There is basic earth wisdom in their taking charge.

The Outside Occasion

The beauty of these variants is that they are all possible. Consumers do want changes. And only through their own Cooperative Funeral Homes can they see their visions take root.

There is always the possibility that private-profit funeral directors, sensing consumer interest in variants, will change their practices and offer more choice. That is splendid. More people—those whom we could never induce to cooperate with us—will have the benefit of our work. They may pay more, but they will have more options. It will be good to know that we have taken benefits to the general community, in fact influencing the quality of life and death.

The Cooperative Funeral Home, responsive to requests from its members, may wish to explore outside occasions.

An outdoor band pavilion, on the back lawn of the Home or perhaps in a special park at a distance, can be the site for funeral occasions. Many people would like outdoor band concerts to mark their departure. Why not? The music, sending its waves across the green lawns and upward among the leafy branches, will sing of a life well spent. The listeners, relatives and friends, hearing the music, will think of their mutual loss, their hearts stirred by music.

Speakers, in a formal program, can mount the steps of the pavilion and conduct traditional or not-so-traditional services. There can be a distribution of ashes in special flower gardens adjacent to the pavilion, in which the notion of life joining life will become vivid for those participating.

Memorial gardens are an excellent idea and will draw response from many advanced consumers. Acres of gray tombstones are not an appealing last place of residence for most people. The distribution of ashes among selected flowers and shrubbery would provide a moving and beautiful occasion. Should cemeteries for earth burials fall within the purview and control of the Cooperative Funeral Home, they could include sections devoted entirely to flowers, which can be made available potted and cut for inside occasions at the Home. A small greenhouse can do the job in winter months. Such cooperative flower-growing can reduce the consumer's dependence on the expensive private-profit florist.

Should a large group of members wish the Home to own land for earth burials, new opportunities will arise. There is no reason why cemeteries should look the way they look. Bodies can be buried without regard to location, if the members wish that to be the practice. Unmarked graves, plotted only on an office wall at the cemetery office, can provide space for the rural beauty we miss in those rows and rows of stones, reminding one of blocks of tenements in a crowded city, or of high-rise apartments in Gotham. As a final housing development most cemeteries focus too much on dead bodies, some members will say. A plot of land can be divided between the stone-raisers and the gardeners, so that choice can be maintained. No one need be kept out, that is the primary rule. Or two plots of distant land, each with a different style and in different directions from the Home, can be owned by the Home.

The chartered bus opens up horizons for outside occasions. Arranged by the Home, a visit to a beach, mountainside or public campsite can provide a lovely way to celebrate someone's life. It could be a special visit to a cherished view, for example, followed by a sit-down picnic. How much better a few hours spent this way than in a dismal funeral parlor, in the old way.

The key to all of this, we have to say, is in the ability of the Home to respond to various wishes and needs. If some group in the Home rejects some idea, they do not have to participate in it. There should be understanding and tolerance in the development of Home programs, lest we move into divisive stances, forcing some members to leave the cooperative and start another one down the street: one Home for conventional cooperators, one Home for radical cooperators. What a loss of energy that would be! What a loss of buying power! Undoubtedly, both would decline, having lost the central spirit of Consumer Cooperation.

Let's think about that gentle mountainside, with that piece of woods someone knew was for sale. Let's leave it untouched, just the way it is. Could it serve some of our members?

It is conceivable that permission could be secured for it to become a place for earth burials. If so, the burial of bodies, uncasketed, in the nooks and crannies of such a site, would give life-strength, a natural fertilizer, lending it the natural beauty that life always gives to life. If such is not possible, it can become a marvelous Co-op Memorial Mountain, the resting place for ashes, the place for memorial tree plantings.

Paths sliced through the deep woods would take the hiker up and down the piney paths. The higher the walk, the greater the view. Little waterfalls, chortling in and out of stony ruts along the way, lend light bubbles to the otherwise motionless scenario. Birds slice song into the hush. The visitor, thinking about a dead friend, would think only good and high thoughts. The mean and the crass would have gone their way, leaving only the reflection of a person's fine deeds, outgoing actions, cheerful ways, touching moments. This wooded cathedral would hold the souls of a countless number of cooperators, unencumbered by the sold-out signs of dismal stone-pocked cemeteries. There would always be room for more on the Memorial Mountain.

The ecology of life would be preserved through such a program. There would be no need, its advocates would argue, for setting aside hundreds and thousands of acres for burial plots. Conservationists, student ecologists, flower-lovers, Johnny Appleseeds could exult in the knowledge that a mountainside would stay forever a shrine to life —through its new role. The gaudy signs of death, the crosses and stars and crypts and angels with arms raised, would be replaced by nature itself, by signs of life.

What a place for spiritual retreats, for seminars, for events related to the thoughtful work of the Cooperative Funeral Home! A lodge, built near the roadway, not cutting into the deeper woods, could house a hundred occasions. Perhaps a single marker, inside the lodge or placed nearby, could hold the names of those whose bodies, ashes or perhaps souls alone have been consigned by survivors to this place of eternal rest.

Parallel developments could occur on a gentle plain, too, with a restful view toward a monumental elm in the middle of the field. Or along a stretch of coastline, whose beach property might become available to the Home. Or by a quiet river or lake. Family pilgrimages of remembrance to such beautiful memory-places could be delightful family picnics.

Food and Liquor

Death brings tension, an inward probing that is hard for most people to absorb. The sense of grief—the strange sorrow that overcomes a group in the midst of mourning—needs relief. Many members of the Cooperative Funeral Home might well inquire into the possibility that a portion of the huge basement (if there is one) be set aside for an eating-and-drinking place. There was a time when private homes were large enough for these occasions, when everyone attending the funeral would join the family for hours of good eating, good drinking and, finally, hearty laughter. Grief finds surcease in the new return to life marked by laughter, whose sounds end our pain and ease our sorrow.

Families whose backgrounds recall these occasions will yearn for them, as they themselves struggle with an understanding of death. Recalling the gatherings, they will intuitively know them to be sound, fulfilling, important. There will be those in the fellowship of the Cooperative Funeral Home who might resist this development, yet it should be explored for the sake of unity. The Home, if it is unable to incorporate such an activity in its building for legal reasons or because of fear of divisions within the membership, might have on its list of cooperating groups a local inn or eatery that would welcome a reserved-party night. The Home, in arranging for the celebration, either in its own facility or outside, for those who feel more whole through its practice, is being true to its mandate to serve its members.

The Home as Educator of Adults

The Cooperative Funeral Home is an educational institution. It is designed to teach, to open up the mind to the reality of death. An active Home, accepting this task, will become engaged in a multiplicity of educational tasks in and out of its facility.

The idea of the cooperative as educator is a variant on the traditional scheme we have outlined. It suggests outreach, not necessarily with a view to drawing members into the cooperative (as in a public-relations or sales program), but with a view to challenging the community to become realistic about death, to become engaged in reevaluation of traditional and prescribed ways of handling it.

Some members emphasizing the Home as educator of adults will think of it as a mission station. It does its service job, but it also sends out missionaries to stir up the natives (philosophically), to arouse new concern, to elevate the insights of an entire community.

At the heart of an educational program there must be books and materials. The Home should be a bookseller, a purveyor of ideas. It might even do some printing and reprinting of materials by some of its members on the subject of death and death practices. A corner of the Home would have the literature in racks, with prices indicated. Some items would be free of charge.

The bookshop would be a resource for anyone, member or not, who wished to pursue the subject. Part of the bookshop might be a lending library, enabling materials to circulate freely among those who might not wish to buy materials or have the funds to do so.

Members of an education committee would develop a program designed to get discussions of death and death practices on the agendas of a hundred or more religious, fraternal and service organizations in the community. People on the committee would do research themselves, enabling them to become resource persons themselves, to sit on panel discussions, to participate in debates, to be interviewed on radio and television.

None of this, it is important to emphasize, is necessarily related to the matter of building up membership. If it happens, that is fine, but the purpose of each individual working on the education committee ought to be (1) the encouragement of advance planning, (2) the public discussion of death and death practices, (3) the nurturing of discussion and study groups in existing organizations, (4) the wider distribution of educational materials on the subject and (5) the spreading of the idea that the Home is an educational resource in the field of death, death planning and death practices.

Members of such a committee, whose work would be truly unique in most communities, will want to spend considerable time with each other and with their books. They will have the expertise, but before they become teachers they must be learners. One by one, as each member reaches out to the community, experiences will return to the group, giving it a boost for yet greater activity.

The committee might wish to develop a master plan for its activity among adults. It should list the various groups in the community, identify those it knows most about (some committee members might also be members of those groups) as well as those it knows least. No group that has monthly meetings, discussions, public events for its membership need be exempt from the list. Death can be a compelling subject for everyone.

A basic service from the committee to the community would be a speakers' bureau type of activity. Hundreds of groups seek thoughtful and good speakers for their meetings; some may actively welcome the committee's unusual concern. Many will refuse interest and decline the opportunity. But momentum develops, always, if the committee does but persist. At some point, in the queer logic of these things, it will become fashionable to discuss death, and then you will not have enough time and energy to handle all the inquiries.

Many communities boast extension or evening schools for adults, sometimes in connection with the public high school or the local community college. The more informed leaders of the committee might consider preparing a syllabus on death education and presenting it to the evening school organizers as a possible course entry. Social workers, religious institutional personnel, teachers, senior-citizen-center staff members, psychologists, doctors, lawyers and ordinary citizens can use such seminar and classroom experiences, for few have been taught even to talk about it themselves, much less talk about it with those asking for help.

If the committee can think of its task as opening up conversations about death wherever it seeks to have input, it will have many rewards. Even where the program might seem too advanced, too sticky, too disturbing for a group's membership, there will have been a conversation. In this sense, every outgoing effort by the committee will be productive. The worst thing that can happen to the committee is that someone will say No, and that is not too dreadful to contemplate. For many people who say No today will wind up saying Yes tomorrow.

The Home as Educator of Children

Begin with the children, some members will advocate, and you have the world. That seems right, if you can get to the children. Unfortunately, they are protected from discussions of death by hovering school officials, parents, clergy and others who are themselves fearful about the subject.

The hard-nosed realism of which children and young people are capable—from elementary school through college—is always a surprise to adults. If children have fear, if they harbor superstitions, they have been reached by nervous adults. Television, particularly, has contributed a cynicism about death which complicates the Home's interests, but even that visual engagement and the resulting hardness can be used to turn discussions profitably to children's own real views about death, their feelings about the death of loved ones, their wishes for themselves.

A committee of the Home which focuses on the education of children may well look to the homes of its members. How can the Home help members in their training of children, particularly the youngest children? Seminars for parents on introducing the idea of death and handling the death experience of children will certainly be welcomed by parents, who have nowhere to turn, most of them, except to their own possibly inadequate backgrounds.

Some public junior and senior high schools have accepted outside assistance in the conduct of classes on death education, sometimes included in social studies. Even English classes have been used, as students have been encouraged to write about death, or to write their own obituaries, thus forcing a personal reevaluation of life. Good idea. Home economics classes discussing consumer problems can well draw on the Home's committee, to discuss the ideas of advance planning, low-cost funerals and the rights of consumers in every aspect of the marketplace.

Conclusion

The Cooperative Funeral Home, like death itself, is a moment in time.

It can be used as a focus for growth. We have to choose how to use it.

By working together, by coming to the point where we recognize that the tasks of death are everyone's, we face death in a new way. We free ourselves from exploitation, from undignified obeisance to old and useless forms. We become a free people.

The idea of a memorial society and its logical extension into the idea of a Cooperative Funeral Home are commended to people everywhere. Beyond the Home is a better society.

Write. Let us know of your experience. By sharing, we will all grow.

Appendix A

QUEENS MEMORIAL SOCIETY

EXPRESSION OF MY PERSONAL WISHES
FOR PROCEDURES AT TIME OF DEATH

I wish to outline my preferences regarding procedures to be followed at the time of my death, namely:

1. CLERGYMAN

That_____ (Church, Synagogue) be contacted immediately in order that my clergyman_____may offer assistance to my family.

2. FUNERAL DIRECTOR

That_____be asked to take care of the requested arrangements as itemized herein.

3. TREATMENT OF BODY

That my body be:

☐ buried in_____Cemetery in_____

☐ cremated and my ashes:

    ☐ buried in _____Cemetery in_____

    ☐ placed in a columbarium in_____Cemetery in

                      city and state

    ☐ disposed of as follows:_____

_____

☐ donated to_____Medical School for anatomical science studies as per previous arrangements, copy of agreement in my personal files.

4. MEMORIAL OR FUNERAL SERVICE

That there be:

☐ a memorial service (without the body) at_____

_____(specify location)

☐ a funeral service (with the body) at_____

_____

☐ a committal service: Private_____ Public_____

☐ no service of any kind

☐ other arrangements, as follows_____

_____

5. MEDICAL RESEARCH AND HUMANITARIAN PURPOSES

That the following wishes be carried out, if possible:

☐ Donation of eyes to The New York Eye Bank
   (Form, completed in advance, and copy in my personal files)

☐ Permission for post-mortem examination (autopsy)

150

6. MEMORIAL DONATIONS OR FLOWERS

That there be donations, as specified, to:

☐ Memorial Fund of_____(Church, Synagogue)

☐ Medical Research Charity_____

☐ Local or National Charity_____

☐ Other_____

That there be:

☐ flowers used at discretion of my family.

☐ no flowers.

☐ no limitations or restrictions as to flowers.

7. OTHER CHOICES OR WISHES (if applicable)

That there be:

☐ private service limited to family and close friends   ☐ public service   ☐ disposal of body, as soon

as legally permissible, in manner indicated at Number 3 above   ☐ closed casket   ☐ open casket

☐ no visiting hours and no display of my body   ☐ visiting hours

☐ obituary notice at the time of death   ☐ embalming

☐ obituary notice prior to a memorial service   ☐ no obituary notices

8. I DESIRE THAT MY CASKET BE MADE OF:

☐ pine   ☐ stained hardwood   ☐ solid hardwood

                    ☐ light gauge metal   ☐ heavy gauge metal

REMARKS_____

_____

_____

_____

I have given careful thought and consideration to the above expressed wishes and have discussed them with my family. I understand that there is nothing legally binding in the above expression and that the ultimate decision is to be made by my next of kin. Nevertheless, I hope that my wishes will be fulfilled, to the extent that they concur with the wishes of my family.

                                                             (Mr.)
                                                             (Mrs.)
_____19____   (Miss)_____

                                                   _____
                                                   number and street

                                                   _____
                                                   city, state and zip code

Copies of this "Expression" may be filed with the Queens Memorial Society, as well as with next of kin, clergyman, or funeral director. Extra copies are available upon request.

The Society assumes no liability, financial or otherwise, in connection with the above instructions.

QUEENS MEMORIAL SOCIETY
Box 53, College Union
Queens College
Flushing, New York 11367

Appendix B

"Putting My House in Order" is an exceptionally fine planning document available from the Continental Association. Section I of the document is essentially advance planning for funerals, including a kind of life history to help your survivors write your obituary. Section II is unusual and of great assistance, for it gives you an opportunity to describe those aspects of your personal property that will need attention. Sets of three are available for $1.00 from the Continental Association and free of charge (to members) from many memorial societies.

However, you can do the job yourself without preprinted forms. Spending a couple of hours reviewing your situation and making extensive notes on the facts of your life can make a great difference to those survivors who will have to conclude your affairs on your death.

Among the items you might wish to record are the following:

Death Benefits: List the associations to which you belong that have death benefits. Your employer, your trade union, your church or synagogue may have a program of that type. Remember the various insurance policies you have that may include death benefits. Remembering these—and noting them —may be of considerable value to your survivors.

Military Service: Note all the details of any military service you may have experienced.

Property Ownership: List carefully all property you own outright or in which you have interest. This can be in many forms, including real estate. Don't forget the castle in Spain you inherited from a distant cousin! And stocks and bonds as well.

Insurance: List all the policies, of all types, you possess, naming the companies, the purpose of the insurance and your local agent's name.

Bank Accounts: List all the accounts, savings and checking, you have and in what banks they are located. Include accounts in credit unions and other organizations.

It is also a good idea to list the liabilities you have, such as bank loans, mortgages, personal notes and the like, for these will be an important factor in handling your estate.

Such a comprehensive personal-planning effort on your part has several benefits: (1) it gives you an opportunity to review your own situation; (2) it simplifies arrangements for your survivors who must handle them; (3) it saves time and energy and may save money your survivors might have to spend on lawyers to figure things out later on; (4) it can give you a sense of pride in having your affairs in order. Needless to say, this planning effort is no substitute for a Will; it is only a helpful addition. Every conscious consumer should have a Will; if you have none, consult a lawyer right away. It can be difficult for your family if you die without one.

Notes

Introduction

1. Jessica Mitford, *The American Way of Death* (New York: Simon and Schuster, 1963).
2. Ruth Mulvey Harmer, *The High Cost of Dying* (New York: Collier-Macmillan, 1963).
3. Leroy Bowman, *The American Funeral* (Washington, D.C.: Public Affairs Press, 1959).

Chapter 1

1. *Consumer Reports* is published monthly by Consumers Union of the United States, 256 Washington Street, Mount Vernon, N.Y. 10550.
2. *Changing Times,* the Kiplinger magazine, is published monthly by the Kiplinger Washington Editors, Editors Park, Md. 20782.
3. *Money* is published monthly by Time, Inc., 541 N. Fairbanks Court, Chicago, Ill. 60611.
4. *Moneysworth* is published fortnightly by Avant-Garde Media, 251 W. 57th Street, New York, N.Y. 10019.
5. Publisher of *Consumer Reports.*
6. The Consumer Federation of America is at 1012 14th Street, N.W., Washington, D.C. 20005.

Chapter 2

1. The *Manual,* in its 6th edition and now entitled *A Manual of Death Education and Simple Burial,* is available from Celo Press, Burnsville, N.C. 28714.

Chapter 3

1. The Movement for a New Society is headquartered at 4722 Baltimore Avenue, Philadelphia, Penn. 19143.
2. The Cooperative League of the USA is located at 1828 L Street, N.W., Washington, D.C. 20036.
3. A listing of Eye Banks is included in *A Manual of Death Education and Simple Burial* (see note 1, chapter 2).
4. The Continental Association of Funeral and Memorial Societies is at 1828 L Street, N.W. Washington, D.C. 20036. Canadian readers will find thoughtful help and guidance in all matters relating to memorial societies from the Memorial Society Association of Canada, 5326 Ada Blvd., Edmonton, Alberta, Canada.
5. The Rockland County Memorial Society is reached at Box 461, Pomona, N.Y. 10970.
6. The Consumers Memorial Society is at 465 Grand Street, New York, N.Y. 10002.
7. *California Co-op Leadership* is printed monthly, October through May, by Associated Cooperatives, 4801 Central Avenue, Richmond, Calif. 94804. Fred Nora is its editor.
8. The San Diego Memorial Society is located at 3656 Eugene Place, San Diego, Calif. 92116.
9. The Bay Area Funeral Society is reached at P.O. Box 264, Berkeley, Calif. 94701.

Chapter 6

1. Joseph G. Knapp has completed two books of his trilogy on cooperative development in the United States: *The Rise of American Cooperative Enterprise, 1620-1920,* and *The Advance of American Cooperative Enterprise, 1920-1945.* They are available from Interstate Printers and Publishers, Danville, Ill. 61832.
2. Farmland Industries is located at 3315 North Oak Trafficway, Kansas City, Mo. 64116.
3. The Information Services Department of Universal Cooperatives is

located at 408 S. First Avenue, Albert Lea, Minn. 56007, and the Head-quarters at 111 Glamorgan Street, Alliance, Ohio 44601.

4. Mid-Eastern Cooperatives is located at 75 Amor Avenue, Carlstadt, N.J. 07072.

5. The Council for Self-Help Development is located at 465 Grand Street, New York, N.Y. 10002.

6. The North American Student Cooperative Organization is located at 2546 Student Activities Building, Ann Arbor, Mich. 48104.

7. The Institute for a Democratic Economy is located at 730 W. Shiawas-see, Lansing, Mich. 48202.

8. Cooperative Services is located at 7404 Woodward, Detroit, Mich. 48202.

9. Information about the Cooperative Institute Association can be secured from Mid-Eastern Cooperatives (see note #4, above).

10. The University Center for Cooperatives is located at Lowell Hall, 610 Langdon Street, Madison, Wis. 53706.

11. Consumers Cooperative of Berkeley, has its office headquarters at 4805 Central Avenue, Richmond, Calif. 94804. Its weekly publication is *Co-op News.*

12. The Family Buying Cooperative Association is located at 202–85 Rocky Hill Road, Bayside, N.Y. 11361.

13. The Queens Consumer Assembly can be reached at Box 53, College Union, Queens College, Flushing, N.Y.11367.

14. The International Cooperative Alliance maintains its headquarters at 11 Upper Grosvenor Street, London W1, England W2X 9PA.

Chapter 7

1. The Cooperative League of the USA, 1828 L Street, N.W., Washington, D.C. 20036, has literature on the direct-charge approach.

2. In addition to the fine bibliography in the *Manual* (see Chap. 2, note 1), readers are referred to Robert E. Neale, *The Art of Dying,* (New York: Harper & Row, 1973).

3. Information is available from the Re-Evaluation Counselling Communities, 719 Second Avenue, N., Seattle, Wash. 98109.

Index

P4